WISER INVESTING

WISER INVESTING

DIVERSIFY YOUR PORTFOLIO BEYOND STOCKS AND BONDS

BENJAMIN C. HALLIBURTON, CFA

ForbesBooks

Published by ForbesBooks, Charleston, South Carolina.
Member of Advantage Media Group.

ForbesBooks is a registered trademark, and the ForbesBooks colophon is a trademark of Forbes Media, LLC.

Printed in the United States of America.

10 9 8 7 6 5 4 3 2 1

ISBN: 978-1-946633-43-9
LCCN: 2018966631

Book design by Megan Elger.

This publication is designed to provide accurate and authoritative information in regard to the subject matter covered. It is sold with the understanding that the publisher is not engaged in rendering legal, accounting, or other professional services. If legal advice or other expert assistance is required, the services of a competent professional person should be sought.

Advantage Media Group is proud to be a part of the Tree Neutral® program. Tree Neutral offsets the number of trees consumed in the production and printing of this book by taking proactive steps such as planting trees in direct proportion to the number of trees used to print books. To learn more about Tree Neutral, please visit **www.treeneutral.com.**

Since 1917, the Forbes mission has remained constant. Global Champions of Entrepreneurial Capitalism. ForbesBooks exists to further that aim by bringing the Stories, Passion, and Knowledge of top thought leaders to the forefront. ForbesBooks brings you The Best in Business. To be considered for publication, please visit **www.forbesbooks.com.**

To my mother for being supportive and encouraging; to my father for being demanding and entrepreneurial; to my brother for pushing me intellectually; to the teachers at McCallie, Vanderbilt, and Duke, whose dedication and knowledge need to be recognized; to the partners at Brundage, Story & Rose for the opportunity to develop as an investor; to my Tradition partners for their work in building our business; to my clients for their trust; to my in-laws for their encouragement; and to my wife, Anne, for being a supportive and loving partner.

TABLE OF CONTENTS

ACKNOWLEDGMENTS

This book would not be possible without the contribution and collaboration of Michael Ciccone, CFP°. Michael helped develop many of our white papers, blogs, graphs, and tables that explained how wiser diversification works. His contribution to the project cannot be understated. In addition, other key members of Tradition Capital Management, LLC's team were heavily involved with certain aspects of creating and editing the book over time. These contributors include Adam Levy; Mary Kelly; Marc Davis, CFA; Heather Mazzouccolo; Patrick Kearney; and two of our summer interns: Robert Raiola and Andrea Ferrell.

I would also like to thank the various asset managers who helped us build these strategies and contributed to our knowledge of various asset classes. Although some of them would like to stay anonymous, I would like to thank them anyway. My specifically named thanks go to Chin Liu, Casey Frazier, CFA, Philip Bartow, and Karan Sood. I would also like to thank Karen Barr and Laura Grossman of the Investment Adviser Association (IAA). In addition, I would like to thank Bob Veres for his significant knowledge of the development of the Registered Investment Adviser industry.

This book also relies on the prior research of various academics and sophisticated practitioners. The key ideas of this book lean on these researchers, and we acknowledge their contribution in our list of sources. Finally, I would like to acknowledge the contributions and hard work of the ForbesBooks and Advantage Media Group team: Bonnie Hearn-Hill, Nate Best, Megan Elger, Kristin Goodale, and Corie Luzon.

DISCLOSURES

STATEMENT OF DISCLOSURES CONCERNING
THIS BOOK AND ITS AUTHOR

Benjamin C. Halliburton is the sole author of this book and is solely responsible for its contents. Neither Tradition Capital Management, LLC (Tradition), nor its employees or members, are responsible for its contents. Though Mr. Halliburton is an owner/member of Tradition, he is not writing or providing any information in this book that is meant to be promotional of Tradition, its services or its investment strategies. Any current of future client of Tradition may or may not utilize, or be advised by personnel of Tradition to utilize, any investment strategy or any asset class or investment direction mentioned in this book. The author recognizes that many factors must be considered in the application of any professional investment management strategy or direction which may be employed for any client, including any strategy or suggestion mentioned in this book. Readers are therefore advised that the contents of this book are for information and education only and are not to be construed as any form of advocacy for the services of Tradition as more particularly described below.

The following is provided as further disclosure concerning the author's employer and its services:

Tradition is a US Securities and Exchange Commission (SEC) Registered Investment Adviser under the federal Investment Advisers Act and provides portfolio management and related services for a fee. Nothing in this book should be considered a solicitation to buy or an offer to sell shares or units of any security, or provide investment-related services by Tradition. Investing in stocks and other assets could result in losses, and positive returns are not guaranteed. Diversification may reduce risks of capital loss but does not eliminate these risks. Expected returns, expected risk, and long-term expected returns are not forecasted returns or risks but are only statistical definitions for modeling purposes. Actual results could vary materially from these returns and could result in losses. Financial assets are also exposed to potential inflation and liquidity risks. Past performance of any strategy or asset class, including any mentioned in this book, or, any strategies and asset classes employed at Tradition at the time of the publication date of this book is not indicative of future results, and all investments could lose value in the future. At a given time, any investment asset class or other forms of investment assets may lose value and result in substantial losses as more particularly described below under Risk Disclosures. Neither the author nor Tradition makes any assertions, estimates, nor guarantees about future results from any strategies and individual assets contained therein.

RISK DISCLOSURES CONCERNING INVESTMENT
ASSETS AND INVESTMENT ASSET CLASSES

Investing in stocks, bonds, and other assets that present various forms of risk to investors could result in losses, and positive returns are not guaranteed. Diversification only reduces risk of capital loss and does not eliminate this risk. Measures of expected return and/or expected risk are not forecasts of returns or risks but are only statistical definitions for modeling purposes based upon financial and statistical analyses. Past performance is no indication of future results, and all investments or assets could lose value in the future due to a variety of financial factors. Due to volatility exhibited in various investment markets, including but not limited to stocks, bonds, and other forms of invest-able assets, including asset classes described in this book, investors are advised that these markets may not perform in a similar manner in the future. Among other risks that can affect value, financial assets are also exposed to potential inflation and liquidity risks. Investors may experience different results in any chosen investment strategy or portfolio depending on the time and placement of capital into any assets associated thereto. The performance of a specific, individual investments may vary substantially from the examples and graphs in this book. Investors are cautioned that they should carefully consider fully diversifying their total personal investment allocations to incorporate a variety of invest-ment assets, which also may include stocks, stock mutual funds and ETFs, international assets, bonds and fixed-income instruments (where appropriate), and other non-stock/bond investments (e.g., without limitation, real estate, reinsurance, alternative lending, timberland, VRP harvesting, real assets, and other asset classes as they have been discussed in this book, or, may be advised or analyzed through other information sources).

The graphs are for illustrative purposes only to show possible return profiles of various asset classes. These illustrations are not historical returns and are not projections of future returns. These illustrations are not compliant with any independent investment performance measurement standards including those of the Global Investment Policy Standards organization and are shown only for illustrative purposes. Mr. Halliburton does not make any assertions, estimates, or guarantees about future results. Future results are unpredictable and could result in losses. Expected long-term returns are not forecasts or guarantees and are merely reasonable long-term goals for diversified strategies. Actual results could vary materially from these expected long-term returns and could result in losses.

For example, and not exclusively among all graphs displayed herein, the "Average vs Compounded Expected Returns & Risk Impact" graph (Figure 7.3) illustrates the difference, for each diversified strategy and the stock-and-bond-only comparable, between the expected average returns and compounded returns of the median result of a Monte Carlo simulation of 5,000 trial twenty-year periods. Over 5,000 random trials of twenty years, half the results should be above and half below the median. This is not a forecast or prediction and is graphically presented for illustrative purposes only.

Many of the asset classes discussed in this book can be accessed through mutual funds and the interval fund subset thereof. Please review the full prospectus of any fund that you are considering. There are no express or implied recommendations or endorsements of any mutual fund, exchange traded fund, any investment vehicle or asset manager employing any strategy in this book, including any firms or individuals who may have been named. These name references are made in the text for commentary and sourcing for definition and explanation of asset classes and strategies only. It does not express or imply any person's or firm's endorsement of any aspects or text within this book, nor this book's endorsement of them. The full range of risks pertaining to any individual fund or asset, and advisory or cautionary disclosures regarding same is beyond the scope of this book. The author's personal or recommended utilization of any strategies or asset classes for deployment within portfolios may change over time and without notice.

ABOUT THE AUTHOR

Benjamin C. Halliburton is a founder and chief investment officer of Tradition Capital Management, LLC. He oversees investment research and strategy for Tradition, heads the Investment Committee, and is the lead portfolio manager for equity strategies. He is also responsible for development of the firm's global strategies and led the firm in diversifying its assets. While he has in-depth knowledge of both the energy and technology sectors, which he has covered as an analyst for nearly three decades, he has also been investing and picking stocks in most sectors of the market during his long investment career.

Since starting his investment career at Merrill Lynch in 1986, Ben has been continuously involved in investing. He managed money while he was earning a master of business administration with a focus on finance from Duke's Fuqua School of Business in 1990, where he was distinguished as a Fuqua Scholar.

Ben continued his investment career with Brundage, Story & Rose (BS&R), where he was the firm's director of research, responsible for overseeing the equity selection process. In recognition of his investment skills, the firm named him a partner. He chaired the Research Committee and was a member of the Investment Policy Committee. Ben developed a valuation methodology that utilizes fundamental, company-specific research to estimate key financial metrics allowing for the prioritization of stock investment opportunities.

He also designed, developed, and managed BS&R's successful Disciplined Growth Strategy, an equity strategy focusing on growth at a reasonable price (GARP) stocks. In 1994, he earned the Chartered Financial Analyst designation.

Ben started to receive some attention and was first quoted in *Barron's* in 1998. He helped found Tradition in 2000 and has been seen on numerous leading national business shows, including *Forbes on Fox,* and programs on CNBC, Bloomberg TV, Fox Business, and the now-defunct Financial News Network. Ben has also been quoted in print and web publications such as *The Wall Street Journal, Bloomberg Businessweek, Financial Times, Market Watch, The New York Times, U.S. News & World Report,* Associated Press, Dow Jones Newswires, and Reuters.

INTRODUCTION

Every serious investor owns equities in their portfolio, either in individual stocks, mutual funds, or ETFs (exchange-traded funds). Some utilize individual bonds, certificates of deposit (CDs), and bond funds to produce income or to diversify and lower expected risk. A few are into real estate or direct private investments in certain companies. More aggressive and adventurous people with spare capital may speculate in cryptocurrencies, futures, options, commodities, derivatives, and other asset classes.

Diversification is a good way to spread risk in your portfolio. Don't put all your eggs in one basket—the eggs being your money, and the baskets being an individual stock or, more broadly, an asset class like stocks or bonds. Most investors diversify into stocks and bonds to decrease overall portfolio risk.

But what if I told you that, while you haven't been doing anything wrong by using just stocks and bonds, you can now obtain wiser investment strategies? Are you missing out on some important keys to building and protecting real wealth? Are there asset classes that you are not utilizing that are typically part of the investment portfolios of institutions like Yale and Harvard, as well as the extremely wealthy?

In this book, you'll learn strategies that can help you build and protect your wealth, produce extra income, and help you secure your future. You'll go behind the curtain and investigate some strategies and tactics used by sophisticated institutions and the gilded class. These are little-known to most investors, but they are the bedrock for investing many family fortunes and those of large institutions. As we dive deeply into them, you'll learn that even though smart investors may be playing a great game with only stocks and bonds, their hand is only utilizing a portion of the available cards in the investment deck. This book will show you the rest of the cards and why they are so important to building wiser, stronger, truly diversified portfolios.

Together, we will examine some of those cards, including reinsurance, infrastructure, agricultural properties like orange trees or vineyards, farmland, variance risk premium (VRP) harvesting, alternative lending, and real estate. These investments are now available to all investors in the form of a specialized subset of mutual funds with a limited liquidity structure, called *interval funds*. These mutual funds were historically unavailable to most investors, but their availability has dramatically increased over the past few years. They represent the missing cards to add to your deck of stocks and bonds. You can now play the game with a full deck, as the big institutions and uber-wealthy have done for years.

THE WISER WAY

Although typically known only by a very select group of investors, these are proven investments that have been used for decades—some for centuries. What has changed is that you no longer have to invest $10 million in a single investment. You can now invest as little as $1,000 in one of these diversifying assets—interval mutual funds. It changes the game. You now have all the cards in the deck, and you can put all the investments into your wiser portfolio. My company is aiming to help every investor achieve their financial goals—investors of all sizes who are now ready to take a more sophisticated approach to building their financial future.

Our strategies can scale down for people who have less than $10 million—in some cases, as little as $50,000—and who haven't had exposure to these wiser diversifying assets in the past. The issue for most of these investors is that they don't know what they don't know. They have no idea that this methodology actually exists, because they've never had it explained before.

You see, these diversifying assets were previously embedded primarily in limited partnerships with million-dollar minimums for each asset class. That precluded the mass market (any investor with less than $10 million) from really getting involved and left these strategies mainly to big institutions and ultra-high net-worth individuals. But times have changed. These assets classes are no longer the exclusive domain of large institutions. The concept of wiser diversification is not hidden behind the walls of major banks and financial services firms, who share these opportunities only with their biggest customers.

Now, investors with as little as $50,000 can take advantage of these strategies and build real, sustainable, compounding wealth. And the good news is, diversifying into these financial admixtures can actually lower overall expected portfolio risk.

This is not meant for the short-term investor. You won't save for a year or two and then use it to buy a house. It's for those with a long-term horizon, which may include an investor paying for a child's college education in ten to fifteen years or for a comfortable and secure retirement, or for someone who may already be retired but is trying to generate higher income, or for the investor creating a legacy for their family.

IT'S NOT MAGIC. IT'S JUST MATH.

How do you manage to build a portfolio with high risk-adjusted expected returns? Two secrets: low-correlation diversification, and illiquidity premium.

First is diversification into low-correlation and uncorrelated assets. Wiser diversification is nothing but math, and portfolio optimization builds more efficient, more optimized portfolios. Generally, the more risk you take, the higher the expected return. However, mixing in assets that are uncorrelated reduces risk through diversification, not by exclusively lowering returns. Portfolio risk can be reduced in two ways: lower return or lower correlation. Inside this book, you'll find an entire chapter that explains the mathematics behind wiser diversification.

The second is what's known as an *illiquidity premium*. All that means is that you get a higher return on your investment if you can't withdraw it quickly, compared to high-liquidity investments. That's one of the reasons real estate, limited partnerships, and private equity funds do so well as investment classes. They invest in assets that have big illiquidity premiums and deliver substantial returns to long-term investors whose need for capital is not immediate.

Keep in mind that interval funds are SEC-registered, '40-Act mutual funds, which have limited liquidity and potentially have gating mechanisms. (Generally, interval funds must repurchase no less than 5 percent of outstanding shares. This is the *gate*, or maximum amount that can be sold by investors in any one period, usually quarterly.) But with that limited liquidity, you do pick up the illiquidity premium along with access to these diversifying assets.

I wrote this book for people who are serious about wiser investing. Yes, it is going to show you some things that sound too good to be true. The goal is to educate you on how diversification works, convince you that there truly is a wiser way to invest, and then have you consider if wiser diversification is something that could help you. I know smart, experienced, professional investors who have told me that it is "too good to be true" in the first moments of our conversation but finish with, "This makes a lot of sense." They often add, "especially with stocks so high" or "with bonds yields so low."

Thank you for choosing to read this book. At a minimum, you will get new information. If I have done my job correctly, you will also be a wiser investor.

Benjamin C. Halliburton, CFA

CHAPTER 1

Bonds are Broken

"An investment in knowledge pays the best interest."

—Benjamin Franklin

ARE YOU A SERIOUS INVESTOR? Perhaps you're nearing retirement and wonder if your portfolio will be able to generate enough income or capital gains to provide for the rest of your life. You may be concerned about the bonds in your portfolio, and you should be. In Figure 1.1, you can see what has happened to bonds over the last thirty-eight years. Back in the early 1980s, yields on the 10-year US Treasury bond peaked at over 15 percent. After that, from 1981 to 2016, bond yields collapsed to less than 1.5 percent. Yes, you read that correctly: the yield on the 10-year Treasury bonds fell by over 90 percent from 1981 to 2016. A portfolio of one million dollars invested in 10-year Treasury bonds in 1981 would have generated an income of $150,000 per year, but that same investment in 2016 would have only generated $15,000 per year.

Bonds—and specifically bond yields, or their ability to produce income—are broken.

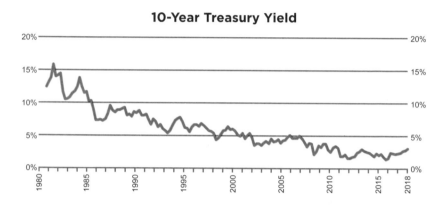

Figure 1.1 a

A similar trend happened with the 30-year treasury bond, as shown below.

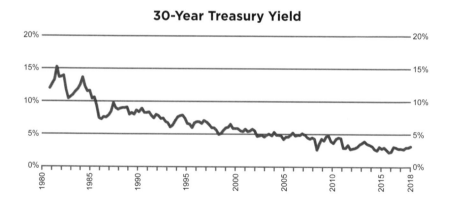

Figure 1.1 b

At the time of this writing, rates have started to move back up from the 1.5 percent level to just over 3 percent. While that improves the yield, existing bond prices go down as interest rates go up; hence, investors who owned bonds as yields went up lost money, because the price of the bond went down more than the yield increased. While the 3 percent yield is an improvement, bond prices will continue to go down as the yield goes up. It is a catch-22.

The graph below shows that bonds are overpriced even compared to stocks. Figure 1.2 shows the historical comparison of the Standard & Poor's (S&P) 500 price-to-earnings (P/E) ratio to the 10-year Treasury bond P/E ratio for the last fifty-six years. The Treasury bond P/E is the multiplicative inverse of its interest rate. For example, a 10 P/E is equivalent to a 10 percent interest rate calculated as follows:

$$1\,/10\% \quad \text{or} \quad 1 \text{ divided by } 10\% \quad \text{or} \quad 1/.1 = 10$$

Investors use these ratios to measure whether an investment is over- or undervalued. If you look at the chart, you'll see the divergence of the S&P 500 P/E and the 10-year Treasury bond P/E from 2008 through 2018. Although stocks as a whole have remained around an average of 20, bonds have had dramatic swings up and down through the third quarter of 2018.

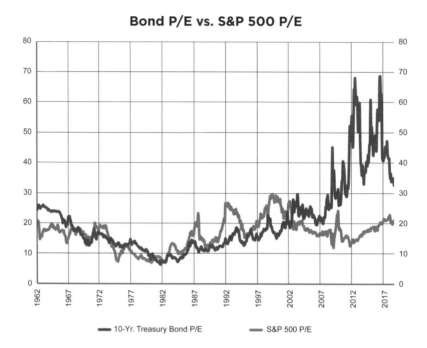

Figure 1.2

There has been much discussion in the financial press about the idea of stocks being expensive compared to long-term averages. Although it is true that stock P/E ratios (as represented by the S&P 500) are in fact moderately above historical averages—currently around 19 for the S&P 500, compared to an average of 16.65 since 1962—this moderately elevated level pales in comparison to that of bonds. At our firm, we feel that bonds are grossly overpriced and potentially in bubble territory, which leads to a question you may be asking yourself: "If stocks are somewhat expensive, and bonds are extremely overpriced, where should I be investing my money?" I wrote this book to answer that and other important questions you may be asking.

In this chapter, we're going to look at evidence to support the fact that bonds are indeed broken. We are also going to examine why they are broken and why they can be risky.

BONDS ARE BROKEN? HOW DID THIS HAPPEN?

That's the first question asked by most people who have invested in once-safe bonds. It happened because the Federal Reserve increased its balance sheet from $800 billion to nearly $4.5 trillion by buying bonds, which drove up prices and drove down yields. (See Figure 1.3.)

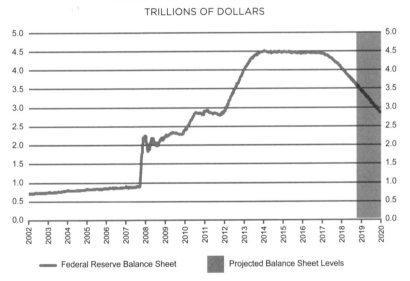

Federal Reserve Balance Sheet
TRILLIONS OF DOLLARS

Figure 1.3

To understand this, let's back up to 2007, when mortgage-backed securities started to show cracks because, as the economy slowed, many of the individuals who had those mortgages began to default on their loan obligations, creating problems for the holders of mortgages and mortgage-based derivatives. As that trend gained momentum, the housing bubble burst, home prices plunged, mortgage defaults escalated, and the owners of those mortgages and their derivatives found limited market for their toxic holdings. This infected the banking system, creating a situation where banks and investment banks were on the verge of bankruptcy. Bear Stearns had to be bought by J.P. Morgan, Lehman went bankrupt, and Merrill Lynch was purchased by Bank of America. Even the mighty Citigroup and Bank of America were on the brink of bankruptcy. It is called BANKruptcy for a reason.

The Federal Reserve came to the rescue, pumping trillions of dollars into the Treasury and mortgage-backed securities markets and lowering interest rates, propping up an economy that threatened ruinous collapse. It was a moment that took down several hundred-year-old investment firms that had bet heavily on derivatives and mortgage-backed securities. That economic stimulus slowed in December of 2013, when the Federal Reserve announced it would taper its bond-buying—that tapering began in January 2014—and its balance sheet peaked in the fall of 2014 at $4.5 trillion.

In 2017, the Federal Reserve indicated it would start to shrink its balance sheet by letting it run off and not buying new bonds. This means as the bonds mature the Federal Reserve is not reinvesting the capital from these bonds. The biggest buyer of bonds, the Federal Reserve, had driven the price up and yields down and artificially set the interest lower than market forces would generally dictate. As a rule, 10-year and 30-year Treasury bonds' yields are close to the nominal gross domestic product growth rate (GDP, a monetary measure of the market value of all final goods and services produced in a period of time).

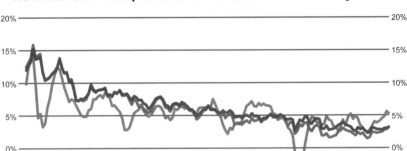

Nominal GDP compared to 10-Yr and 30-Yr Treasury Yields

GDP is Gross Domestic Product, a measure of US economic activity

Figure 1.4

As I write this book in 2018, the nominal GDP growth is estimated to be around 5 percent for the year, and both 10-year and 30-year Treasury bond yields are just over 3 percent. I believe yields will go up as the big buyer, the Federal Reserve, stops buying. This means bond prices will go down as yields go up. The mix of higher yields and lower prices means total return on bond investments will remain low for the next five to fifteen years as yields and prices move to market-based, not Federal-Reserve–manipulated, prices. I expect total returns for bond investors to be in the range of 1.5 percent to 3.5 percent, depending on the speed with which rates and yields rise and prices fall. That's a major trouble spot for the bond market. Who will buy those Treasury notes and bonds? That situation could lead to a sell-off in 10-year and 30-year bonds. Many investors have yet to realize what is clearly evident on the charts. I want to emphasize that I do not know the timing of the increase in interest rates, but I do know rates will probably go up as market forces take over.

BONDS ARE RISKY

When an investment fails to yield enough to protect your capital, that investment is risky. Today, in addition to their low yield, bonds carry the risk of higher interest rates. Figure 1.5 illustrates the risks of holding onto a bond as interest rates go up; specifically, it shows the bond price losses that would be incurred. Low yield and high interest rate risk is not really a sound investment.

Loss in Treasury Bond Value Percentage
CURRENT TREASURY YIELD INCREASED BY 1%, 3%, AND 5%

Treasury Bond	Yield	1%	3%	5%
2-Year	2.85%	-2%	-6%	-10%
3-Year	2.94%	-3%	-8%	-13%
5-Year	3.01%	-5%	-13%	-20%
10-Year	3.16%	-8%	-22%	-34%
30-Year	3.34%	-17%	-41%	-56%

This table shows the approximate price gain or loss in the 2, 3, 5, 10 and 30 year Treasury notes or bond if yields were to move up from today's yields by 1%, 3% and 5% immediately. It does not include coupon as part of total return. Nor does it include time as a factor for the move. The yield change is assumed to be instantaneous. Yields as of September 30, 2018.

Figure 1.5

Moreover, this means that bonds are not going to provide retirees with enough income to sustain their lifestyles, however fiscally conservative those lifestyles may be. In fact, once you factor in inflation, those bonds are basically break-even propositions and will cost you significant capital if rates go up as I envision. You are right to be concerned that you are going to lose money by staying with bonds, because if you do so, you will be locking yourself into a long-term, low-interest base. Without another capital resource, you could spiral downward.

Another more technical way to look at bonds is their duration, which is a measure of interest rate risk. As interest rates have moved down over the past several decades, a perverse increase in duration or interest rate risk has accompanied this decline. Yes, you read that correctly. As interest rates came down, the risks went up, meaning lower return and higher risks.

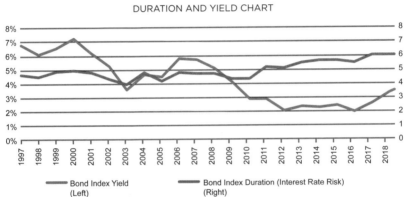

Bloomberg Barclays Aggregate Bond Index

DURATION AND YIELD CHART

Bond Index Yield (Left)

Bond Index Duration (Interest Rate Risk) (Right)

Figure 1.6

That's why bonds are not only broken but are a risk now and in the near future. They are no longer generating enough income to meet your needs. You can imagine how it feels to realize, after investing in bonds for up to thirty-six years, that you will receive nothing close to 15 percent and indeed something closer to 3 percent.

HYPOTHETICAL CASE STUDY: JUSTIN
AND SERENE—RETIRED

Here's a possible example of what can happen when one depends too much on bonds for income and security. Over their working years, Justin and Serene had saved approximately $1.5 million with a standard portfolio mix of stocks and bonds. Upon retirement, when Justin was seventy and Serene was sixty-eight, they decided to move from New Jersey to Florida and change their portfolio to only fixed income to increase its income yield. In addition to their combined twenty-year life expectancy of 54 percent, there is a one-in-ten chance that one of them will still be alive and in need of income in twenty-nine years.

Joint Life Expectancy Table for a Couple
at Age 70 (Male) and 68 (Female)

THE PROBABILITY OF AT LEAST ONE BEING ALIVE IS 54%, 25%,
AND 10% IN 20, 25, AND 29 YEARS, RESPECTIVELY.

			Probability of Living		
Years	Age - M	Age - F	Male	Female	Either or Joint
20	90	88	21%	42%	54%
25	95	93	6%	21%	25%
29	99	97	2%	9%	10%

SOURCE: SOCIETY OF ACTUARIES RETIREMENT PARTICIPANT 2000 TABLE

Figure 1.7

Although the cost of living in Florida was significantly lower than in New Jersey, Justin and Serene still needed approximately $90,000 every year for their living expenses. With interest rates so low, they were able to generate only about 3 percent yield from their typical, fixed-income portfolio of bonds and CDs. This created an income shortfall, because the portfolio's income was only $45,000. This shortfall forced them to take about $45,000 in capital out of their portfolio every year and spend it to supplement the interest income and cover living expenses. This capital reduction reduced the portfolio's ability to produce income in subsequent years. The next year, the portfolio only had $1,455,000, and a yield of 3 percent generates only $43,650, which means the couple had to take $46,350 out of the portfolio to get the $90,000 needed for living expenses. The "run out of money death spiral" had begun. The situation is even worse, because living expenses will go up with inflation. The all–fixed-income portfolio is doomed to failure in the current low-interest rate world.

Once you start depleting capital, you go into a financial death spiral. The portfolio generates less interest and dividend income, so every year, you're taking more and more out of it—something you just can't do. I can't emphasize enough how important it is, especially given the longer life expectancy that people have today, that they— you—not take more money out of the portfolio than it generates, not even a little bit, before you're in your eighties. If you start taking capital in addition to earnings out of the portfolio too early, you will wear the portfolio down too fast, and you will be spending those retirement years you planned for dealing with a great deal of stress and loss of security.

WILL YOU OUTLIVE YOUR MONEY?

Although the hypothetical couple in our case history is a composite, the story of what happened to Justine and Serene is all too real for many people, and solutions are not easy to find unless one knows where to look. In a 2017 survey, 65 percent of Americans said they lose sleep over financial concerns.[1] That is only four percentage points fewer than the number of Americans who had money-related insomnia in 2009; these figures are notably higher than in 2007, just prior to the recession and housing crisis, when 56 percent of Americans were losing sleep over financial worries.

A 2014 *Reuters* article written by Chris Taylor shows that 22 percent of those interviewed said they would rather die early than not have enough cash to live comfortably in retirement.[2] On that same note, Allianz conducted a survey showing that 77 percent of people in their late forties worried more about outliving their money in retirement than about dying itself. Interesting to note is that the percentage rose among those who were married with dependents. Of those respondents, 82 percent said that running out of money was a more chilling prospect than death. These statistics indicate how important providing for the future is for many Americans and how much they worry about it—perhaps more than they worry about dying.[3] It's no surprise that those with dependents were more worried about outliving their money. Providing a cushion for those we leave behind is a major reason many people invest.

Justin and Serene are a hypothetical example of people who invested the right way, based on what they understood about investing. However, they relied on the traditional methods of building that worked when interest rates were higher. They invested in stocks and bonds. They owned their own home. They adopted a

---

1   Brady Porche, "Poll: 2 in 5 Americans lose sleep over health care costs," credit-cards.com, https://www.creditcards.com/credit-card-news/losing-sleep-money-worries-poll.php.

2   Chris Taylor/Reuters, "Is Outliving Your Savings a Fate Worse Than Death?" Time Money, http://time.com/money/3581647/retirement-savings-outlive-death-worse/.

3   "The Allianz *Reclaiming the* Future Study White Paper," Allianz, https://www.allianzlife.com/-/media/files/allianz/documents/ent_991_n.pdf.

relatively frugal lifestyle. They rotated into bonds to try to maximize income in their retirement. No one advised them to consider another way to protect themselves financially and prepare for a secure future. To be fair, when they started investing, the alternatives shared in this book would not have been available to them. Today, these diversifying assets are available to them and to you as well.

DIVERSIFYING ASSETS TO IMPROVE EXPECTED YIELD

Justin and Serene could use diversifying assets in conjunction with stocks and bonds to improve the income coming off their portfolio, creating a situation where they did not have to dip into their capital every year. Most investors fail to take advantage of the additional expected return and wealth-building attributes of investments that have longer horizons. Investments that do not offer daily liquidity (that is, are not available for quick sales) earn an extra expected return called an ***illiquidity premium***: the lower the liquidity, the higher the extra expected return. Although all investors need some liquidity, they will need most of their money in decades or at least years down the road, and they could take advantage of the illiquidity premium. As noted earlier in this book, interval funds are mutual funds that take advantage of this illiquidity premium. Justin and Serene didn't know about these strategies.

In conjunction with stocks and bonds, diversifying assets should be able to provide around a 6 percent expected return (expected yield combined with expected capital appreciation), most of which could be achieved with income yield. If they had taken this approach, Justin and Serene could have generated $90,000 of retirement income from their $1.5 million-dollar portfolio without needing to draw down their initial capital to supplement their living expenses in most years.

If the capital base was not depleted, its ability to produce for future years would be maintained. This would make it much more likely that Justin and Serene would not run out of money in their retirement years.

Their current strategy of using fixed-income investments and CDs is viewed by many as safe, but unfortunately it is doomed to failure in the current low-interest-rate environment, because it is not producing a high enough income or expected return stream to cover retirement living expenses. When that happens, the only apparent escape is to deplete capital.

Now you can see that bonds no longer work as a singular investment, because their yields are too low, hence, they don't generate enough income for the investor. Bonds are thus riskier than many investors believe. A typical investor's portfolio is composed of mostly stocks and bonds, such as with the very common 60 percent stocks and 40 percent bonds mix. With the Barclays Aggregate Bond Index producing an expected yield of 3.6 percent and the S&P 500 having a current dividend yield of under 2 percent, this investment strategy is likely to produce very little income for a portfolio.

It is not impossible to achieve a decent level of income from your portfolio. However, it appears that the days of being able to do so by investing only in US Treasuries and investment-grade corporate bonds are at an end.

Fortunately, there are other uncorrelated or low-correlation assets classes that can be introduced into a portfolio to lower volatility while providing a higher expected yield. The low-interest-rate environment we have experienced for most of the past decade has made it extremely difficult for investors to generate income, but it is not impossible to achieve a decent level of income from your portfolio. However, it appears that the days of being able to do so by investing only in US Treasuries and investment-grade corporate bonds are at an end. One solution is to look at alternative income-producing investments to achieve a higher expected yield while maintaining a similar level of overall investment portfolio risk.

Our firm has developed just such a strategy, which we will explore further in later chapters, to provide our clients with a higher expected income despite the low-interest-rate environment. Positioned as an income component within a globally diversified portfolio, this income segment can reduce the amount allocated to low-yielding fixed-income investments; thus, the portfolio has the potential to improve a client's expected income stream compared to a traditional, bond-only portfolio. Because we are believers in diversification, we advise clients to utilize these diversifying assets in conjunction with stocks and bonds.

This strategy is designed for investors seeking higher yields than bonds and with similar volatility but less interest rate risk. Our strategy uses assets with low correlation to achieve high income for clients while controlling risk through diversification. The utilization of truly low or uncorrelated assets such as reinsurance, private real estate, alternative lending, timberland, infrastructure, and VRP harvesting strategies to increase yield and diversification has a profound effect on portfolio risk reduction. The strategy has a current expected return (expected yield combined with expected capital appreciation) of approximately 6 percent with the bulk of that being expected income yield.

THE BOTTOM LINE

The bottom line is this: Bonds are currently broken, and if you expect to have a retirement that is sustainable and comfortable, you need to understand that brokenness and alter the traditional approaches that have served generations before you. I started this chapter by asking if you are a serious investor and if your portfolio is sustainable enough to generate income or capital gains to provide for the rest of your life. I also asked if you were concerned about the bonds in your portfolio. I hope that, after reading this chapter, you are, because if so, you are now ready to examine another, potentially better, way.

———————————— Your Takeaway ————————————

- Bonds are broken and a poor investment. In thirty-seven years, their yield has dropped from 15 percent to around 3 percent.

- The Federal Reserve broke bonds when it increased its balance sheet from $800 billion to almost $4.5 trillion buying bonds, driving up prices and driving down yields.

- Bonds have the dual problem of paying you very little and being very risky if rates go up.

- Retirees depending on bonds to finance their retirement may find themselves having to deplete their capital.

- Excellent additional choices are available. Using diversifying assets could be a solution.

CHAPTER 2

Diversification: The Only Free Lunch

"The doors of wisdom are never shut."

—Benjamin Franklin

IT'S LONG BEEN SAID THAT DIVERSIFICATION is "the only free lunch" in investing, a quote attributed to Nobel Prize laureate Harry Markowitz. I like to put it this way to my clients: If you're using only stocks and bonds to build a portfolio, you're utilizing a small fraction of the available investment universe. As shown on the following pie charts, domestic equities and bonds are a fraction of the investable universe.

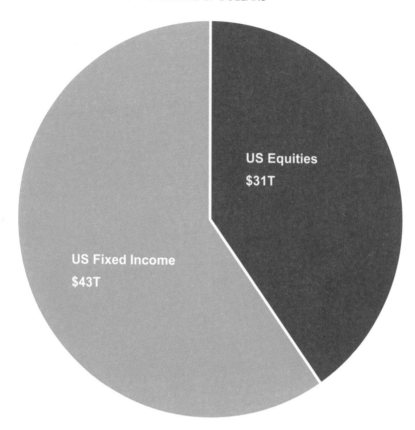

US Equities and Fixed Income
TRILLIONS OF DOLLARS

US Equities
$31T

US Fixed Income
$43T

SOURCE: STONE RIDGE, ILLUMINATING THE PATH FORWARD

Figure 2.1

United States Equities and Fixed Income represent only a portion of the global market for stocks and bonds as shown in Figure 2.2.

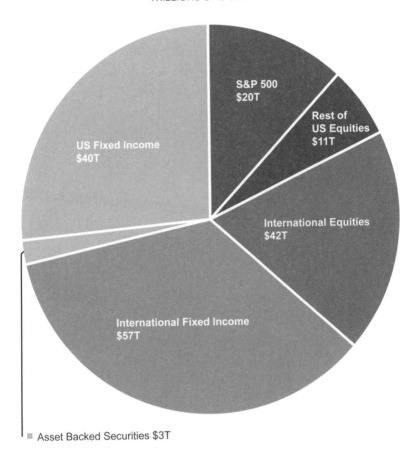

Global Equities and Fixed Income
TRILLIONS OF DOLLARS

S&P 500
$20T

Rest of
US Equities
$11T

US Fixed Income
$40T

International Equities
$42T

International Fixed Income
$57T

■ Asset Backed Securities $3T

SOURCE: STONE RIDGE, ILLUMINATING THE PATH FORWARD

Figure 2.2

In turn, global equities and fixed income represent only part of all the global investment asset classes.

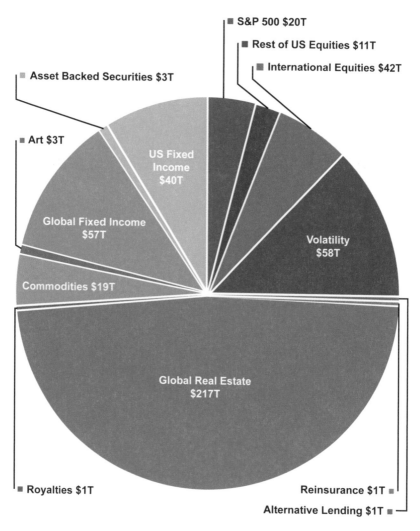

Global Asset Classes
TRILLIONS OF DOLLARS

SOURCE: STONE RIDGE, ILLUMINATING THE PATH FORWARD

Figure 2.3

Figure 2.3 shows you the available investment opportunity set and how US stocks and bonds are only a small part of that opportunity set. To too many investors, US stocks and bonds make up the only opportunity set, and people—maybe you—don't realize there are other places to invest their money.

Let me walk you through the top of the chart. A total of $31 trillion is available in US equities, and $43 trillion is in US fixed-income assets. And then you can see the rest of the trillions of dollars of assets available.

This chart shows that US stocks and bonds—what the bulk of US investors choose—are a very small part of the investable universe, and you can see that many other opportunities exist that you may not have considered before. If you were playing cards, you would be playing with a partial deck. Is this where you are, currently? Now, let's imagine that you're playing that same game but that you're holding all the cards in the deck, not just a few. This is what happens when you are dealing with the full investment opportunity set with all the asset classes.

The key to diversification is using more assets. The less correlated those assets, the better. Ray Dalio, of Bridgewater Hedge Fund, referred to diversification as the "Holy Grail of Investing" in his book, *Principles*. Traditional diversification involves adding more assets at relatively high correlations. Wiser diversification is adding uncorrelated and low-correlation assets. Adding one uncorrelated asset (two assets in the portfolio) can reduce risk by 29 percent. Utilizing six uncorrelated assets reduces risks by nearly 60 percent.

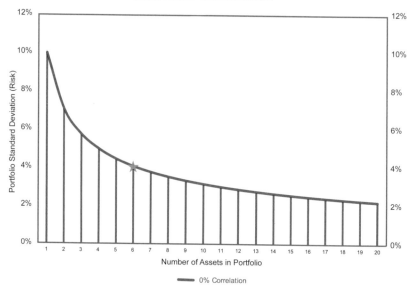

Portfolio Risk Reduction from Adding Assets with Zero Correlation

Figure 2.4

Dalio wrote, "From my earlier failures, I knew that no matter how confident I was in making any one bet I could still be wrong—and that proper diversification was the key to reducing risks without reducing returns. If I could build [a portfolio filled with high-quality return streams that were] properly diversified (they zigged and zagged in ways that balanced each other out), I could offer clients an overall portfolio return much more consistent and reliable than what they could get elsewhere."[4]

If you look at the chart above, you can see why Dalio called it the "Holy Grail of Investing." Indeed, it was an impressive claim. Now, I am going to explain to you why these statements are true. Figure 2.4 shows you the gist of why this diversification works. On the purple line, we're mixing in together assets that are uncorrelated

---

4   Ray Dalio, *Principles* (New York: Simon & Schuster, 2017).

(the real world is more complex, but a correlation of zero more easily displays the concept). If you have one asset, it is a modest risk of 10 percent standard deviation (risk) as shown on the vertical axis, and it has an assumed 7 percent expected return. If you have two assets, your risk goes down. If you have three, it goes down again. If you have four, it goes down again. If you have six assets in a class, you're basically reducing the risk from 10 percent to 4 percent.

To put it in perspective, the stock market has about a 15 percent to 16 percent risk number (volatility). The bond market has about 5 percent expected volatility. So, in this simplified example, we're showing a mid-level, 10 percent risk item and assuming a 7 percent expected return. Stocks are considered riskier. So, in this example, we're showing a mid-level, 10 percent risk item. But the key thing is here, we can take six 10 percent risk items that are uncorrelated and have 7 percent expected returns. We mix them together, and the risk goes down 60 percent, while you still keep that 7 percent expected return. *The return does not go down as you mix in diversifying assets with higher expected returns as it would with low-yielding bonds.*

HOW MANY BOATS ARE YOU TRUSTING TO DELIVER YOUR MONEY?

Most people ride the ups and downs of the market, moving things around as needed and generally trying to stay abreast of the constantly changing circumstances of business and the financial markets. If they're smart, lucky, and/or have knowledgeable advisers, they get a decent return on investment. However, if the stock market hits an iceberg, and investors are just moving their stock funds, ETFs, and individual stocks around, those assets are essentially all in the same boat.

If the boat goes down, the investments all go down. The uber-wealthy and big institutions are not keeping all their money in one boat. They have already split up their assets into multiple boats that are navigating different courses to the destination. If you do the same, and one of those boats is delayed or damaged, you still have reasonable results. That is the wisdom of diversifying assets. You need to have some of your money in other boats. Wiser diversification is simply a better way to generate income, protect your portfolio, and compound at a faster expected rate than you can get by staying only in stocks and bonds.

> That is the wisdom of diversifying assets. You need to have some of your money in other boats.

HOW DIVERSIFICATION WORKS

The concept of uncorrelated or completely independent asset classes is difficult to understand. We have prepared a graph that we believe helps explain the process. We have set up simplified assets that assume 0 percent correlation, or complete independence. (The real world does not quite operate like that, but to explain the concept, we have made this simplifying assumption.) This is the same assumption we made in Figure 2.4.

Thus, we have taken six assets with the exact same expected return (7 percent) and the exact same risk (10 percent) and run them as independent outcomes. These assets' values are displayed as colored lines on Figure 2.5. As you can see, the outcomes vary dramatically depending on the simulation's random future events, even though all the assets have the exact same expected returns and risk. However, if you have a portfolio that holds all six of these assets in an equal proportion for twenty years, as shown here, the portfolio value changes are much less extreme, with less zigzag, and the return is more predictable. The thick black line shows this diversified value below. We have assumed seven distinct investments of $100,000— six single-asset portfolios for each of the six assets and one portfolio combining all six assets, equally weighted—each projected over twenty years.

Moreover, the return from the combined six-asset portfolio is much more stable and has much smaller losses than any of the individual asset portfolios has on its own. The randomly generated returns for the diversified six-asset portfolio generated a maximum loss of $1,852 in any one year. On the other hand, the worst loss of any single asset in one year was $40,508, and the single-asset portfolio with the smallest single-year loss still generated an $11,288 loss in its worst year. Diversification with uncorrelated assets allows an investor to build a portfolio that has smaller overall drawdowns and more stable, predictable returns.

To look at this another way, we have graphed the seven portfolios' year-to-year percentage changes. As you can see, the colored lines zig and zag all over the place and are very volatile with little predictability. However, the combination portfolio, while still experiencing some variation, creates a more stable and predictable return, as shown with the black line.

Wiser diversification is nothing but math. It builds more efficient and better optimized portfolios. Generally, the more risk you take, the higher the expected return. However, wiser diversification mixes *uncorrelated* assets, and therefore it is able to maintain average returns while still lowering the overall expected portfolio risk. Often, when I explain this to investors, they think it's too good to be true. However, if you do the math, you can see how to build a portfolio with better risk-adjusted expected returns.

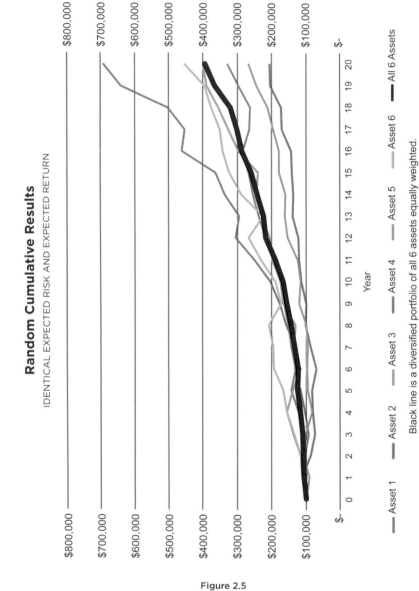

Random Cumulative Results
IDENTICAL EXPECTED RISK AND EXPECTED RETURN

Year

— Asset 1   — Asset 2   — Asset 3   — Asset 4   — Asset 5   — Asset 6   — All 6 Assets

Black line is a diversified portfolio of all 6 assets equally weighted.

Figure 2.5

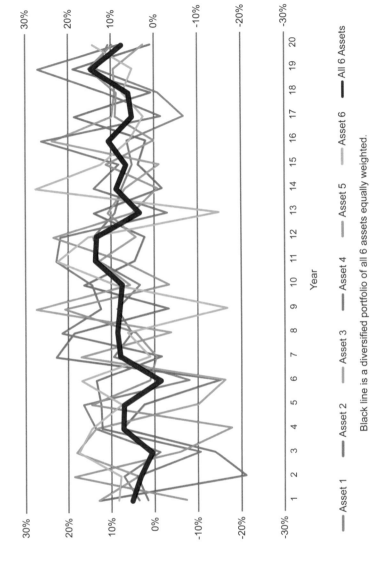

Random Annual Percentage Return
IDENTICAL EXPECTED RISK AND EXPECTED RETURN

Asset 1 — Asset 2 — Asset 3 — Asset 4 — Asset 5 — Asset 6 — All 6 Assets

Black line is a diversified portfolio of all 6 assets equally weighted.

Figure 2.6

ILLIQUIDITY PREMIUMS

Illiquidity premium simply refers to the fact that if you neither need nor want to be able to withdraw your investment quickly, you get a higher return on it. That's why some limited partnerships and private equity funds do so well. They invest in things that have big illiquidity premiums and deliver substantial returns to long-term investors whose need for capital is not immediate.

I'll explain diversification in greater detail in Chapter 7. Right now, I want to assure you again that these are not new, untried asset classes or investments. These asset classes can be found in SEC-registered, '40-Act mutual funds, called *interval funds*, which have limited liquidity on a monthly or quarterly basis and potentially have gating mechanisms that further restrict a fund's liquidity. (Generally, interval funds must repurchase no less than 5 percent of outstanding shares. This is the *gate*, or maximum amount that can be sold by investors in any one period, usually quarterly.) With that limited liquidity, you do pick up some of the illiquidity premium and access to these diversifying assets.

WHAT'S IN THE PORTFOLIO?

So, what's the best strategy for your portfolio? Some of the suggested investment items are familiar stocks and bonds, and others may be unfamiliar to you. However, these wiser diversification strategies reduce risk, are safer than an all-stock portfolio, and are a proven way for investors to see expected returns that could make a big difference in results down the road.

Over the past few years, my firm has been working to build a suitable way to reduce our exposure to low-yielding bonds. Realizing that bond yields are not generating enough income and that exposure to rising interest rates makes them risky, we began implementing our ideas in earnest in 2016. Our bond reduction segment uses diversifying assets, including infrastructure, agricultural land, reinsurance, alternative lending, timberland, VRP harvesting, and investment real estate to increase potential expected return or reduce expected risk through diversification. We'll explore each of these in future chapters, and when you finish reading this book, you should have a strong understanding of diversifying assets, what they are, and how they can work for you. Diversifying assets' independence is what makes them work better, together.

We strive to create a strategy to increase expected yield, not just in the short run but for as long as interest rates remain unusually low. Keep in mind, diversification *reduces* risk of capital loss, but it does not *eliminate* these risks. Past performance is no indication to future results, and all investments could lose value in the future.

TESTED STRATEGY

Wiser diversification provides a higher expected return at every level of risk. The new interval mutual funds gave us access to diversifying assets with much lower investment minimums—$1,000 instead of $1,000,000. We can now help all our investors, not just our biggest ones. We can help our clients retire more securely, invest for their children's college education, increase portfolio income, and simply feel more secure with a portfolio that fluctuates far less than the stock market.

When we first started offering diversifying assets to clients, the new interval funds did not have track records. It took a sophisticated investor who could look at the asset class and figure out what was a reasonable expected return versus expected risk and correlation with other assets. While some tools and data were available, an investor had to make numerous assumptions based on asset classes, their expected returns and their expected risk.

So now that you understand a little more about what you might have been missing in the investment world, let's take a look at some of the ways you can leverage these diversification strategies to your advantage. As you might suspect, there are different asset allocation strategies for investing based on your personal circumstances, your goals, and your timeline for achieving those goals. But all the asset allocation strategies benefit from taking a broader view, getting broader access, and possibly getting a better risk-adjusted expected return, and that's what diversification is all about.

The sooner you start planning for college, buying a house, or investing for retirement, the better off you are. The amazing impact of compounding interest adds significant value to your portfolio. In the United States, we live in a society that often takes a very short-term view of many things. Contrast that to many foundations, institutions, and international cultures, where a hundred-year outlook is often the norm. That's the model we need to adapt here, because tomorrow arrives sooner than we expect. You need to be prepared for what's certain, and what's certain is that you will need funding for your retirement years. Think about how long you and your spouse might live, before you retire and start drawing your Social Security income, not after you retire. In this current low-return environment, you are doing a great job if you're getting a 6 percent expected return on your savings and investments; however, you have to adjust your expected return for inflation (let's assume around 2 percent). That means you get a 4 percent payout after inflation, or real return. Let's say you're taking that 4 percent out to live. If you want to live on $100,000 over and above Social Security or pension payments, you need $2.5 million in savings to avoid dipping into capital on an inflation-adjusted basis. That's why you should start considering wiser diversification through the use of interval funds to access low-correlation asset classes with higher risk-adjusted expected returns and yields. Let's examine interval funds in greater depth and see why they make sense to all investors and not just the extremely large ones.

INTERVAL FUNDS: A CLOSER LOOK

Interval funds can invest in assets that can't be found in typical, open-ended mutual funds and ETFs, and these assets hold great value. These include such tangibles as forests and farmland, both of which produce goods for sale that can be extremely profitable. Interval funds are a way to purchase an interest in such properties without buying 5,000 acres and having to handle their management.

Interval funds carry the all-important illiquidity premium mentioned earlier, which means you can't redeem your shares on a daily basis, but you receive an additional bump in your return for foregoing that privilege. Beyond their ability to invest in diversifying assets, interval funds also offer benefits unique to their structure; the limited liquidity feature means that they offer periodic liquidity, often through quarterly or monthly redemptions. Generally, interval funds must repurchase no less than 5 percent of outstanding shares. This is the *gate*, or maximum amount that can be sold by investors in any one period, usually quarterly. The process is more cumbersome than selling a daily liquid fund, because shareholders (or their advisers) must send a notice of the upcoming redemption intention before a specific deadline to participate in redemption or sell on a future date. Additional gates sometimes place extra constraints or limits on desired liquidity at any one redemption date. For example, across all owners of one specific interval fund, only 5 percent of total capital could be withdrawn on one redemption date.

While all of that sounds like a big negative, in reality, the interval fund structure is a huge positive. It allows investors access to asset classes that are not daily liquid. Investors have to be long-term with these allocations because they may not be able to sell if everyone else is trying to sell at the same time. Unlike open-ended mutual funds and ETFs, interval funds will not be forced to sell assets that are temporarily depressed in a period of investor panic. Make no doubt about it: investors do panic, and there will be a panic in the future.

In such a panic, interval fund shareholders will benefit in two ways. First, they will not be able to panic and sell. Second, the remaining interval fund shareholders will not have the value of their fund marked down by forced selling of illiquid, hard-to-sell assets at panic-driven low prices. These benefits are huge. Investors in typical, open-ended mutual funds and ETFs can sell their shares at any time. As a result, they are susceptible to panic and emotional liquidation at the worst possible time. When markets fall—which they will—investors in open-ended funds and ETFs may panic and sell their shares at a loss instead of remaining committed to their long-term investment plan.

> Interval fund shareholders will benefit in two ways. First, they will not be able to panic and sell. Second, the remaining interval fund shareholders will not have the value of their fund marked down by forced selling of illiquid, hard-to-sell assets at panic-driven low prices.

The other big benefit of interval funds is access to asset classes that are themselves illiquid and are often the best low-correlation diversifying assets. As a bonus, the underlying assets have an illiquidity premium.

As of late 2017, the SEC had registered more than fifty-five interval funds carrying more than $17 billion in assets. Some of them were familiar assets, like farmland. Others were lesser known, such as credit and hedge funds. These funds, which are generally considered "alternative" investments, are growing in popularity as others, such as bonds or publicly traded real estate investment trusts (REITs), are losing some of their appeal.

Unlike certain investments, interval funds are not blind pools of capital. You can generally see what is in the portfolio before investing your money, so there is significant transparency. However, this does not mean that a fund manager will not change investments at any time to optimize the portfolio as long as it meets a fund's mandate.

The individual investor in interval funds gains the advantage of investing in funds that are managed by large investment management companies, but individuals do not have to meet the qualifying net worth or income tests that institutions face.

In legal terms, interval funds are classified as closed-end funds, but they differ from the more traditional and well-known type of closed-end funds that trade in the secondary public markets on the New York Stock Exchange or NASDAQ. Interval fund investors trade directly with a fund through repurchase offers. Interval funds make quarterly or monthly repurchase offers to shareholders, buying back shares from investors based on the price at the repurchase date. Shareholders can either accept or reject the

> The individual investor in interval funds gains the advantage of investing in funds that are managed by large investment management companies, but individuals do not have to meet the qualifying net worth or income tests that institutions face.

offers without penalty. If you decide to cash in your interval fund shares, the price on a repurchase is determined by the per-share value on a specified date at the close of business. For that service, some interval funds take a redemption fee from the proceeds, which is then paid back to the fund. There may be other fees as well, depending on the individual fund. This information will be contained in a fund's prospectus.

Interval funds are regulated by the Investment Company Act of 1940, particularly Rule 23c-3, which outlines repurchase rules. Interval funds are also covered by the Securities Act of 1933 and the Securities Exchange Act of 1934, so there's nothing "too good to be true" about them. These are well-regulated funds.

The beauty of interval funds is that they give all investors access to underlying asset classes that were once only available in limited partnership form. The interval fund structure has been around for a while but was not really utilized for regular, small investors, because creating them was a significantly more cumbersome than regular stock or bond mutual funds. However, to get exposure to each of these additional diversifying asset classes, some asset managers decided to try to roll out these specialized interval funds.

One of the first popular interval funds opened in the real estate sector in 2012. Basically, it was allowing investors to participate in the private real estate sector via an interval fund. A reinsurance interval fund was launched in 2013. Others soon emerged, including one that specialized in VRP harvesting or capture, a strategy that is best delivered in an interval fund or a limited partnership. Then, in the summer of 2016, the same company created an alternative lending fund. After that, other companies followed into those asset classes with interval funds of their own.

The creation of these interval funds was not prompted by a regulatory change. It was simply a matter of focused asset managers finally delivering diversifying assets in a mutual fund structure— the interval fund. These companies were generally built to provide better access to investing in diversifying assets. These fund managers democratized the investing landscape by allowing smaller pools of money to participate in wiser diversification with low and uncorrelated asset classes. The environment for interval funds could not have been better. Interest rates were collapsing, and the asset classes in these funds could often provide better yield and diversification. The end result is that now there are many asset managers rolling out interval funds. Had interest rates stayed at their higher, previous levels of 7–12 percent, I am not sure these changes would ever have occurred.

WHAT DOES IT TAKE TO GET INVOLVED AS AN INVESTOR IN INTERVAL FUNDS?

It varies per fund, but most have a $1,000 minimum. The reality is that I would not advise a client with a total of $1,000 to put it into an interval fund for reinsurance or alternative lending. If this is your entire savings, you probably won't have the liquidity you may need in an emergency. You also have to have a certain amount of capital to give yourself proper diversification. So, for anyone who has less than $25,000 to invest, I advise getting started by building an equity portfolio. You're going to have to live with a little volatility in the stock market, but time has proven that stocks are a reliable long-term investment and a way to build up capital.

At my firm, we ask for a $50,000 minimum investment for our diversified global strategies that include interval funds with alternative diversifying assets. We came up with that number to account for any transaction costs and clients' need for liquidity. It provided us with enough capital to operate and deliver diversification to our clients (if all goes as planned). Generally, we tell our clients under that $50,000 threshold that we'll get started in more liquid investments and then ease into more diversified, low- or limited-liquidity investments.

I would never suggest that somebody put all of his or her money into limited-liquidity investments. Life is unpredictable, and it is impossible to know what events may create a need for liquidity.

HOW MUCH LIQUIDITY?

That brings up another important point that clients ask about all the time. How much of an investment portfolio should be illiquid? That will depend on your time horizon for retirement, college, or other needs. But it's never really about how illiquid it *should* be. It's about how much liquidity you anticipate you will need at any one time or in the immediate future.

As you get older or nearer to college payments, you will need more liquidity than when you are younger and have longer time horizons for your investments. There's little need when you are younger for lower returns in exchange for liquidity. It's time to make your money work hard for you. A younger investor could have about 80 percent of his or her capital in illiquid investments. That doesn't make sense from an economic standpoint, but that younger investor could have that much, and it wouldn't be a problem.

Someone older, though, would probably not want to have more than 50 percent of his or her portfolio illiquid. If you had set up a fund for college, you need to make sure liquidity is increasing as college starts and is completely liquid by the beginning of junior or senior year at the latest. We generally stay well below these theoretical maximums in interval funds, but my point is that most people can have plenty of limited-liquidity diversifying assets, because most of their other investments will provide more than enough daily liquidity.

WHICH INVESTMENTS?

Another common question that we get from our clients concerns how we choose what investments to recommend. Although the future, and returns specifically, are unpredictable, looking at how asset classes relate and work together is a valuable process that helps us build better portfolios. The expected returns and expected risks are not forecasts. They are essential tools as we strive to build portfolios that have strong expected risk/expected return profiles.

One of the positive aspects of a portfolio with minimum drawdowns is the psychological impact on the investors. If they are having smaller drawdowns, they are not pushed into the pressure situation where they're asking themselves (and us), "Do I need to be selling to prevent any further losses?" That's where the uncertainty of the financial markets can cause people to make bad decisions. When times are good, it seems as if they will never end. When times are bad, it also seems as if they will never end.

Understand that you can *dampen* your losses. You are not going to *eliminate* them. Your investments are going to go down when the market goes down, but the diversified strategies should go down far less than the stock market in general, which will allow an investor to stay calm, with losses that are bearable, and be in a position to participate in the recovery. It's just a better way to sleep at night. The reciprocal is also true. When the stock market is booming, a diversified portfolio will almost always lag behind a 100 percent stock portfolio and could lag behind the old-fashioned 60 percent stocks and 40 percent bond balanced portfolio if both stocks and bonds have a good year at the same time.

Over the past few years at Tradition, we have been working to build a suitable strategy to reduce our exposure to bonds, for the reasons I have already stated. So, is diversification the only free lunch? In a nutshell, at every level of risk, by using diversifying strategies, you can pick up a couple of extra percentage points in expected return versus the expected return of a portfolio of only stocks and bonds. As shown below, if you have stocks and bonds, you can mix them to build an efficient frontier. If we diversify into all the assets we outline in this book and utilize global stocks and bonds, we get a new efficient frontier that is above and to the left of the US stock-and-bond-only efficient frontier. You can choose a combination of lower expected risk, higher expected return, or a little of both. Used properly, that strategy is better than a free lunch.

In the coming chapters, we'll examine a few of the asset classes, strategies, and tactics that we recommend to our clients who are seeking a way to broaden their investment portfolios. In Chapter 3, we'll start with an asset class and a concept you may not have heard about: reinsurance.

Diversified Strategies

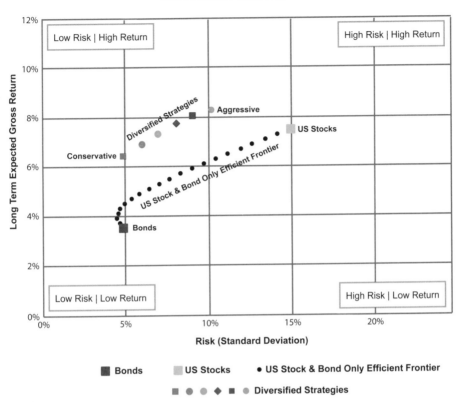

Figure 2.7

Your Takeaway

- Wiser diversification is the better way to generate income, protect your portfolio, and compound at a faster expected rate than you can get by only staying in stocks and bonds.

- Diversifying assets have higher expected returns than bonds in the current environment.

- Diversification lowers overall portfolio risk.

- At every level of risk, by using diversifying assets, you can pick up a couple of extra percentage points of expected return compared to a balanced stock/bond-only portfolio.

- Diversifying assets include infrastructure, agricultural land, reinsurance, alternative lending, timberland, VRP harvesting, and private real estate to increase yield and lower risk.

CHAPTER 3

Reinsurance

"Tell me, and I forget. Teach me, and I remember. Involve me, and I learn."

—BENJAMIN FRANKLIN

YOU ALREADY KNOW WHAT IT'S LIKE to be on the buyer's side of insurance, correct? Basically, you pay for insurance in the hopes that you never need it, but you are glad you have it when you need it. Until you do, you see each premium payment as just another expense.

When you invest in reinsurance as an asset, you're taking the other side of that transaction. In that scenario, you are going to *receive* premium income in exchange for taking on the risk that a claim is made in the future. As the insurer providing that risk insurance, you know that you are going to get the premium, but you do not know when—and if—a claim is going to be made. As a result, there is an unpredictable return stream from your investment. In general, this return stream will be the premiums, net of any claims. However, in really bad years, the claims will be in excess of your premiums collected, and you are going to have to pull money out of your capital to pay those claims, resulting in a net loss for the year.

As you can see, it's just the opposite side of the very familiar consumer transaction of paying that monthly insurance premium.

A PROVEN INVESTMENT OVER TIME

One question people often ask me when we first discuss reinsurance is, "How long has it been around?"

My answer: "A long time."

Then, I go on to explain that reinsurance has been around thousands of years, and it can be traced back as far as 3000 BC, when the Babylonians devised a system of maritime loans as a way of dealing with huge financial risks. The Code of Hammurabi released the borrower from having to repay the loan in case of accidents. Ancient Chinese merchants used numerous ships for their cargo instead of gambling on only one for safe transport. That was an early version of what we now call *diversification*.

In those days and for centuries beyond, the shipping industry was the primary focus of insurance. Ships were expensive to build, required constant maintenance, endured the ravages of weather and piracy threats, and carried cargo that itself represented a substantial investment. When a ship went down or was plundered, multiple parties sustained substantial losses.

Around 916 BC, Rhodes is credited with creating a system of maritime law wherein any losses incurred were settled on the basis of the "general average," which means that one person's losses were divided among several groups with a stake in the venture. People would buy insurance on their ships and their cargo in case the ships sank or were pirated. The first recorded reinsurance contract, which was issued in 1370, covered a ship sailing from Genoa to Bruges, located in the province of West Flanders in what is now Belgium.

By the late 1300s, larger risks were beyond any one insurer's capacity. Thus, the practice of *coinsurance*—where an insurance company would shop its risk to other potential insurers—came into being. It was the earliest form of reinsurance. Carriers that wanted to get on board with the project would sign their name under the description, "underwriting" the risk. The first appearance of the actual term "reinsurance" dates to 1457, preserved for history in a legal document from Florence, Italy.

Risk management evolved from there. The American Revolution, from 1775 to 1783, created further changes. Businesses were cut off from their former insurers, so new insurance companies formed in the former colonies that became the United States.

Understandably, tragedy seemed to precede these early reinsurance companies. Following the Great Fire of Hamburg in 1852, Cologne Re, the first independent reinsurance company, began business. After a large fire in Glarus that destroyed two-thirds of the town, the predecessors of UBS and Credit Suisse formed Swiss Re in Zurich in 1863.

Around 1885, Cuthbert Heath at Lloyd's sold the first excess of loss reinsurance. Then came the San Francisco earthquake of April 1906, one of the most significant earthquakes of all time. Following that devastation, the reinsurance market demonstrated its ability to fund catastrophic losses.

Then the reinsurance companies started approaching institutional investors and other reinsurance companies that basically said, "Hey, let's swap our risk. So, I've got too much European storm risk, and you've got too much Florida hurricane risk. I'll take a little of your Florida. You take a little of my European storm. We'll swap

Then the reinsurance companies started approaching institutional investors and other reinsurance companies that basically said, "Hey, let's swap our risk. So, I've got too much European storm risk, and you've got too much Florida hurricane risk. I'll take a little of your Florida. You take a little of my European storm. We'll swap those out, and then, we'll have a lower total portfolio risk."

those out, and then, we'll have a lower total portfolio risk." And with that, they started swapping. In short, they started selling to institutional investors, and then the limited partnership structure appeared in the mid-1990s, followed by the mutual fund structure in about 2014. Today, we face different challenges and risks, but reinsurance continues to be an important diversification tool.

THE GREAT DIVERSIFIER

"Reinsurance by its very nature is uncorrelated," says Chin Liu, managing director at Amundi Pioneer. "In its natural state, it is going to have a return stream based on the occurrence of catastrophes across the world. This has very little to do with financial markets and so is uncorrelated with these financial markets. This makes reinsurance a great diversifier."

The reinsurance mutual fund investor puts in the capital, and then the mutual fund puts that capital into a trust that is supporting reinsurance risk. So, in exchange for risking the possibility that someone will file a claim, the reinsurance fund receives the premium the consumer pays as it comes into the fund. However, if a claim is made, it is repaid out of the premiums first. If necessary, the claim can also be paid with principal or capital invested by the investor, creating a loss for the investor.

Reinsurance was one of the methods Warren Buffett used to build his fortune. In 1967, Buffett's company, Berkshire Hathaway, bought National Indemnity, its first reinsurance business. It later bought General Re, another very large reinsurance company.

As we've already discussed, diversification is mixing together low-correlation or uncorrelated investments, and if you mix six of those diversified (uncorrelated) investments in your portfolio, you reduce risk by 60 percent. This doesn't mean that each individual investment is low risk. It means that portfolio risk reduction is done through the power of wiser diversification, not simply trading lower risk for lower returns. Reinsurance is not a low risk investment, but it is a great diversifier.

In a low-loss year, you can get a return from reinsurance investments in the low teens, somewhere around 10–13 percent. During years like 2017, in which an unusually large number of hurricanes and fires resulted in a big loss year, your returns move into negative territory. In general, we estimate that your returns will average out to about 7–8 percent, but returns will be bumpy and not smooth for reinsurance.

Basically, reinsurance sets up a new asset class. Your investment is based on claims for catastrophes, not on anything to do with the financial markets or the economy. When we have a storm in Houston or a major earthquake in San Francisco, that's when things can get taxing and stressful for the reinsurer.

The risk owned by the reinsurance company is based on probabilities, so the return profile is pretty similar to stocks. It might be a little bit lower risk, but it also doesn't have as high of an upside return in the occasional great years. The risk associated is with the catastrophes, where they are, the exposure, and the size. Let me give you an example of the type of reinsurance investments that are available.

The September/October period in 2017 for the reinsurance funds saw losses because we had Hurricane Harvey and Hurricane Irma both destroy billions of dollars in property. Both happened within a very short timeframe, so there were drawdowns and negative returns in the reinsurance funds in that sector in that time frame.

Fortunately, the reinsurance funds purposefully diversify their exposure via the global reinsurance market. Some of the larger reinsurance risks or perils include Florida wind, Gulf winds, California earthquake, Japan earthquake, and European winter storms. Other exposures include aviation, crops, and other storms and earthquakes across the globe. Reinsurance mutual funds can have rather complex investment structures, as shown in the simplified schematic in Figure 3.1.

Basically, the funds will have exposure to whatever is in the market for reinsurance. They are not actually trying to make active bets one way or the other. They're trying to get diversification and broad exposure to the entire reinsurance market, just as investing in a fund that tracks the S&P 500 Index would give an equity investor exposure to the US stock market.

These instruments allow insurance risk to be transferred to the capital markets in the form of fixed income or other securities. They are packaged in varying formats that allow for customized portfolio exposures, such as catastrophe (CAT) bonds, industry loss warranties, quota shares, and collateralized reinsurance.

This asset class provides investors with attractive diversification properties and potential risk-adjusted returns. These outcome-oriented investments are great diversifiers, because they have low correlation to the financial markets. Instead, their performance is linked to non-financial events such as hurricanes and earthquakes.

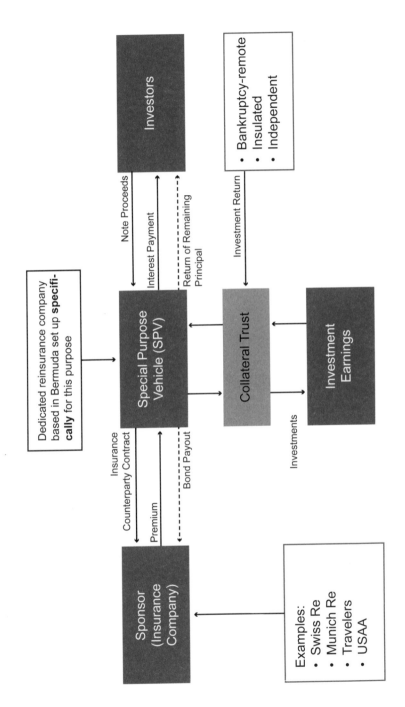

Figure 3.1

FORMATS

Here are the key characteristics of CAT bonds, collateralized reinsurance, industry loss warranties, and quota shares.[5]

Catastrophe bonds, or CAT bonds—These bonds have a precise-level protection above a certain trigger. They are characterized by an active secondary market/144A bond structure; low-frequency, high-severity events, with many having probabilities of occurrence, on average, of 1 in 75 to 1 in 200 years; and a multiyear contract. They offer a strong return potential for long-term investors.

Collateralized reinsurance—These are characterized by customizable exposures across regions, perils, and risk layers; exposure to insurer underwriting risk; a lack of a secondary market; and once-a-year liquidity.

Industry loss warranties (ILWs)—These are characterized by customizable exposures across regions, perils, and risk layers. Loss is not insurer-specific and is calculated by industry-wide loss. ILWs are usually one year or shorter in term and have limited transferability via the insurance broker market. After an event, investors can expect quicker resolution.

Quota shares—These shares feature embedded leverage and thus, efficient use of capital. An investor buys a portion of insurance book and shares gains and losses. Characteristics include one- to two-year terms, once-a-year liquidity, a broadly diversified portfolio, and a more gradual loss curve as opposed to more binary payout.

The funds we utilize invest in quota share notes. Quota share notes are subject to the same risks discussed herein for CAT bonds. In addition, because quota share notes represent an interest in a

---

5   "Redmond Reinsurance Investment Interval Fund," US Securities and Exchange Commission, July 1, 2015, https://www.sec.gov/Archives/edgar/data/1636058/000119312515243167/d889411dn2a.htm.

basket of underlying reinsurance contracts, a fund has limited transparency into the individual underlying contracts and therefore must rely upon the risk assessment and sound underwriting practices of the issuer and a fund manager. Accordingly, it may be more difficult for the investor to fully evaluate a fund's underlying risk profile and therefore place a fund's assets at greater risk of loss than if the adviser had more complete information. In quota share trades, a fund cannot lose more than the amount invested.

Reinsurance-related securities risk—The principal risk of an investment in a reinsurance-related security is the occurrence of a triggering event. These include natural events (such as a hurricane, tornado, or earthquake of a particular size and magnitude in a designated geographic area) or non-natural events (such as a large aviation disaster) that can cause a fund to lose all or a significant portion of the principal it has invested in the security, as well as its right to additional interest payments with respect to the security.

If multiple triggering events that affect a significant portion of the securities held by a fund occur, a fund could suffer substantial losses, and an investor will lose money. A majority of a fund's assets will be invested in reinsurance-related securities tied to natural events for which there is inherent uncertainty as to whether, when, or where they will occur. There is no way to predict with complete accuracy whether a triggering event will occur, and because of this significant uncertainty, reinsurance-related securities carry a high degree of risk.

Event-linked bonds—Event-linked bonds are a type of CAT bond that carries large uncertainties and major risk exposures to adverse conditions. If a trigger event, as defined within the terms of the bond, involves losses or other metrics exceeding a specific magnitude in the geographic region and time period specified therein, a fund may lose a portion or all its investment in such security, including accrued interest and/or principal invested. Such losses may be substantial. Because CAT bonds cover "catastrophic" events, which, if they occur, will result in significant losses, CAT bonds carry a high degree of risk of loss and are considered "high yield" or "junk bonds." The rating primarily reflects the rating agency's calculated probability that a predefined trigger event will occur. Thus, lower-rated bonds have a greater likelihood of a triggering event occurring and causing a loss to a fund.

Risk-modeling risk—Fund managers will generally consider risk models (created by independent third parties, the sponsor of a reinsurance-related security, or a broker) with respect to a funds' investments. Risk models are designed to assist investors, governments, and businesses in understanding the potential impact of a wide variety of catastrophic events and allowing such parties to analyze the probability of loss in regions with the highest exposure. Fund managers will use the output of the risk models before and after investment to assist in assessing the risk of a particular reinsurance-related security or a group of such securities. A risk model uses the most current available scientific and statistical data to estimate the losses that could be sustained due to a catastrophic event, but even the most sophisticated models cannot predict actual losses. Risk models are used by fund managers as one input in the risk analysis process for fund investments.

Illiquidity and restricted securities risk—To the extent consistent with the repurchase liquidity requirement of an interval fund, a fund may invest in illiquid securities. Liquidity risk is the risk that the reinsurance-related securities held by a fund may be difficult or impossible to sell at the time that the fund would like or at the price that the fund believes the security is currently worth. As a relatively new type of financial instrument, there is limited trading history for reinsurance-related securities, even for those securities deemed to be liquid.

Valuation risk—The funds we utilize are subject to valuation risk, which is the risk that one or more of the securities in which the funds invest are priced incorrectly due to factors such as incomplete data, market instability, or human error. In addition, pricing of reinsurance-related securities is subject to the added uncertainty caused by the inability to accurately predict whether, when, or where a natural disaster or other triggering event will occur. A funds' investments in reinsurance-related securities for which market quotations are not available will be valued pursuant to procedures adopted by the board.

Moral hazard risk—Reinsurance-related securities are generally subject to one or more types of triggers, including so-called *indemnity triggers.* An indemnity trigger is based on the actual losses of the ceding sponsor—that is, the party seeking to diversify its insurance portfolio. Reinsurance-related securities subject to indemnity triggers are often regarded as being subject to potential moral hazard, because such reinsurance-related securities are triggered by actual losses of the ceding sponsor, and the ceding sponsor may have an incentive to take actions and/or risks that would have an adverse effect on a fund.

Limited availability and reinvestment risk—Investments in reinsurance-related securities may be limited, which may limit the amount of assets a fund is able to invest in reinsurance-related securities. The limited availability of reinsurance-related securities may be due to a number of factors, including seasonal concentration of issuances, limited selection that meets a funds' investment objective, and lack of availability of reinsurance-related securities in the secondary market.

Reinsurance industry risk—The performance of reinsurance-related securities and the reinsurance industry itself are tied to the occurrence of various triggering events, including weather, other natural disasters (e.g., earthquakes), and other, non-natural, large catastrophes. Triggering events are typically defined by three criteria: They are an event; they must occur in a given geographic area; and they must meet or exceed a threshold of economic or physical loss caused by the event, per a method to measure such loss. Generally, the event is peril of a kind that results in significant physical or economic loss. Natural perils include disasters such as hurricanes, earthquakes, windstorms, fires, and floods. Non-natural perils include disasters resulting from human activity, such as commercial and industrial accidents or business interruptions. Major disasters in populated areas (such as in the cases of Hurricane Katrina in New Orleans in 2005 and Superstorm Sandy in the New York City metropolitan area in 2012) or related to high-value insured property (such as plane crashes) can result in significant losses, and investors in reinsurance-related securities tied to such exposures may also experience substantial losses. If the likelihood and severity of natural and other large disasters increases, the risk of significant losses to reinsurers may increase.

Borrowing risk—The funds we utilize may borrow to meet repurchase requests or for investment purposes, such as to purchase additional portfolio securities. A funds' borrowings, which would be in the form of loans from banks, may be on a secured or unsecured basis and at fixed or variable rates of interest. A funds' ability to obtain leverage through borrowing is dependent upon its ability to establish and maintain an appropriate line of credit. The cost of borrowing may reduce a funds' return.

Leveraging risk—The funds we utilize may borrow or enter into derivative transactions for investment purposes, which will cause the funds to incur investment leverage. Therefore, the funds are subject to leveraging risk. Leverage magnifies a funds' exposure to declines in the value of one or more underlying investments or creates investment risk with respect to a larger pool of assets than a fund would otherwise have. This risk is enhanced for a fund because it invests substantially all its assets in reinsurance-related securities.

Derivative investments risk—The funds we utilize may obtain event-linked exposure by investing in, among others, event-linked swaps, which typically are contingent or formulaically related to defined trigger events, or by pursuing similar event-linked derivative strategies. Trigger events include earthquakes, weather-related phenomena, and other criteria determined by independent parties. If a trigger event occurs, a fund may lose the swap's notional amount. As derivative instruments, event-linked swaps are subject to risks in addition to the risks of investing in reinsurance-related securities, including counterparty risk and leverage risk.

Below-investment-grade securities risk—The funds we utilize can invest without limit in reinsurance-related securities that are rated below investment grade, which are commonly called "junk bonds" and are bonds rated below BBB- by Standard & Poor's Ratings Services or Baa3 by Moody's Investors Service, Inc., or have comparable ratings from another rating organization. The rating primarily reflects the rating agency's calculated probability that a predefined trigger event will occur.

Therefore, securities with a lower rating reflect the rating agency's assessment of the substantial risk that a triggering event will occur and result in a loss. The rating also assesses the reinsurance-related security's credit risk and the model used to calculate the probability of the trigger event. The rating system for reinsurance-related securities is relatively new and significantly less developed than that of corporate bonds and continues to evolve as the market develops. There is no minimum rating on the bonds in which a fund may invest. A fund may also invest without limit in reinsurance-related securities that are unrated and judged by a fund manager to be of below-investment-grade quality.

Credit risk—The funds we utilize invest in reinsurance-related securities which will be subject to credit risk. The principal invested in a reinsurance-related security is held by the special purpose vehicle (SPV) in a collateral account and invested in various permissible assets set forth under the terms of the SPV. Typically, the collateral account is invested in high-quality US government securities—that is, US Treasury bonds. However, in certain reinsurance-related securities, the collateral account may be invested in high-yielding, higher-risk securities. In such instances, a fund will be subject to the risk of nonpayment of scheduled principal and interest on such collateral account investments.

Foreign investing risk—The funds we utilize may invest in reinsurance-related securities issued by foreign sovereigns and foreign corporations, partnerships, trusts, or other types of business entities. Because the majority of reinsurance-related security issuers are located outside the United States, a fund will normally invest significant amounts of their assets in non-US entities. Accordingly, a fund may invest without limitation in securities issued by non-US entities, including those in emerging market countries. Certain SPVs in which a fund invests may be sponsored by non-US-ceding insurers that are not subject to the same regulation to which US-ceding insurers are subject. Such SPVs may pose a greater risk of loss, for example, due to less stringent underwriting and/or risk retention requirements. A fund's investments will consist primarily of event-linked bonds and quota share notes, which provide a fund with contractual rights under the terms of the issuance. While the contractual rights of event-linked bonds and quota share notes are similar whether they are issued by a US issuer or a non-US issuer, there may be certain additional risks associated with non-US issuers.

WHAT ABOUT MAJOR CATASTROPHES?

Given the inevitability of a Gulf storm or a California earthquake, it may seem that the longer you leave your money in a reinsurance fund, the more likely it is that you will sustain a loss. Again, that is not the case when you are dealing with diversification.

There is no way to accurately predict the timing of a major catastrophe. With reinsurance, you receive a reasonable return in years when there is no catastrophe. In a year, when several major disasters occur, the insurance companies are hit, and they must make up for the shortfall. Just as with your automobile and homeowner's insurance, if someone makes a claim, the rate will often increase. In the same way, you can anticipate an expected normal loss year return from reinsurance to increase the year after catastrophes.

> Just as with your automobile and homeowner's insurance, if someone makes a claim, the rate will often increase. In the same way, you can anticipate an expected normal loss year return from reinsurance to increase the year after catastrophes.

With that said, the truth is that in some years, the claims are going to be well in excess of your premiums, and you could lose anywhere between 10 percent and 25 percent. And then, one out of every hundred years, you should expect to lose more than 50 percent. The risk profile for investing in reinsurance is very similar to the risk profile for investing in stocks. Most years you make money, but, on occasion, you do lose a lot of money.

CAN YOU LOSE ALL YOUR MONEY?

The answer is yes. All the money that you have in this particular investment, that is. Yes, you could lose it all. That would be a once-in-a-thousand-years event, but it is possible that there could be massive catastrophes across the globe in any one year that eat up all your capital, and you have a 100 percent drawdown.

As unlikely a scenario as that is, it is definitely possible. It would probably be closer to 90 percent, but that is basically all. That is not that much different than stocks. Within the past one hundred years, there was a 90 percent drawdown in the stock market during the Great Depression. Back in 2009, we had an over 57 percent drawdown. Any time you're trying to get any more than a T-bill return, you're taking on risk, and in this case, you're taking on a risk that is providing you a high expected return, but it is doing so in an uncorrelated fashion with regard to the rest of your portfolio. When you mix it together, your total portfolio risk is less than if you had it all in stocks.

Based on current news about global warming and hurricane intensity, some fear that the rein-surance companies are going to lose money. The reality is that the insurance companies are pricing their products to take into account the fact that hurricane frequency and intensity may be increasing. Insurance companies are pricing the product to make money, period. If the consumer public knows that hurricane intensity and frequency are increasing, I can assure you the insurance companies have known that for some time. You, the investor, are sitting on the same side of the table as the insurance companies.

SOCIALLY RESPONSIBLE INVESTING

Chin Liu, Managing Director at Amundi Pioneer, whom I quoted at the beginning of this chapter, also points out that reinsurance is also an investment that helps people in their times of greatest need. Thus, even when you must occasionally pay more than your premiums, you know where that money is going. "In addition, buyers of reinsurance funds can earn an additional benefit in knowing that when they lose money, their capital is going to good causes to help people rebuild and save lives," Liu says. "Truly socially responsible investing."

———————— Your Takeaway ————————

- Reinsurance is the great diversifier.

- In exchange for risking the possibility that someone will file a claim, the reinsurance funds receive the premiums the consumer pays.

- Reinsurance is uncorrelated with financial markets.

- Unlikely as it is, it is possible that there could be massive catastrophes across the globe in any one year that could eat up all your capital, and you would have 100 percent drawdown.

- Should you lose money, you know your capital is going to save lives and help people rebuild.

WISER INVESTING

CHAPTER 4

Real Assets: Infrastructure, Real Estate, Timberland, and Agriculture

"Energy and persistence conquer all things."

—Benjamin Franklin

REAL ESTATE. INFRASTRUCTURE. FARMLAND. TIMBERLAND.
In your portfolio, you have financial assets, and you can also have real assets. Rather than financial contracts that entitle you to equity, debt notes, and/or bonds, real assets are physical assets that you purchase. You can buy them directly if you have millions or tens of millions of dollars, or you can buy them indirectly through interval funds. These assets have similar benefits and risks in that they are real assets, participate in economic growth, and get some benefits from inflation.

"Real assets have been a primary source of wealth accumulation and preservation for more than five thousand years, but until recently, they have not been available to the average investor," said Casey Frazier, CFA, chief investment officer, Versus Capital Advisors LLC. "These asset classes have historically provided high risk-adjusted returns with low correlation to traditional equity and fixed income markets coupled with solid inflation protection. We believe, as many institutional investors do, that these investments should be a long-term, foundational position in every investor's portfolio."

The risk to these assets is a poor economy that results in or from deflation. However, including them in a diversified portfolio allows you to protect capital and minimize losses during equity market downturns. This is the power of diversification. The benefit is that real assets have similar return structures and low correlation to equity. The power of diversification is that expected returns will be similar to equity returns, but—as you can see illustrated on the chart—the risks will be lower over the long term than with an all-equity portfolio.

Trailblazing pioneers in private real asset investing include insurance companies, pensions, foundations, endowments, and sovereign wealth funds. In the last fifty years, each of these asset classes has become more established within the institutional investor community, where previously it was primarily just insurance companies that invested in real assets while other institutional investors stayed with stocks and bonds. Real estate was established as a common investment class in the mid-1970s, timberland in the mid-1980s, farmland in the late 1980s to the early 1990s, and infrastructure in the late 1990s to early 2000s.

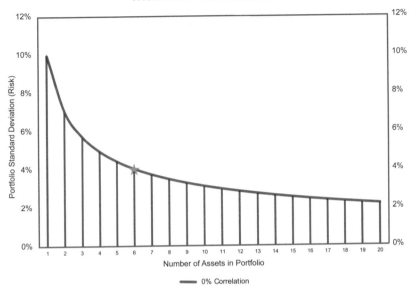

Portfolio Risk Reduction from Adding Assets with Zero Correlation

Figure 4.1

GLOBAL INFRASTRUCTURE

Infrastructure provides facilities and services supporting economic productivity. Transportation, energy, and telecommunications are the three main categories, and they contain many subcategories.

- Transportation assets, including toll roads, airports, seaports, and railway lines

- Regulated assets such as electricity, gas, water distribution, and waste water collection and processing facilities

- Renewable energy, such as hydroelectric, wind, solar, and geothermal

- Communication assets, including broadcast and wireless towers and satellite networks

- Social infrastructure, such as schools, hospitals, prisons, and courthouses

These assets share a stable and predictable income and cash flow, and in many cases, the rates (the fees charged to end users) that are charged by infrastructure assets are determined by regulators, concession agreements with governments, and long-term contracts. Asset owners can usually increase such rates at some level linked to inflation or economic growth.

Much like property, infrastructure boasts a strong performance history. As the United States and other countries begin to update their aging infrastructure systems, the sector should continue to deliver strong performance as an investment.

REAL ESTATE

Real estate, like infrastructure, represents hard assets. Similar to infrastructure, it acts as a strong inflation hedge and offers attractive dividend yields. And, over the past sixteen years, real estate and infrastructure have had had similar average annual returns and low to moderate correlations to other asset classes.

A July 19, 2017, *Forbes* article states, "The iron is hot when it comes to real estate investing. Over the past five years, both residential and commercial real estate have rewarded investors with annual returns greater than 7%. What's more, current home ownership rates are declining, and residential and commercial vacancy rates are also declining, reflecting the fact that the total pool of renters is increasing."[6]

---

6   Marc Prosser, "Data Proves REITs Are Better Than Buying Real Estate," *Forbes*, July 19, 2017, https://www.forbes.com/sites/marcprosser/2017/07/19/data-proves-reits-are-better-than-buying-real-estate/#b9d6809d6b7d.

Over time, real estate tends to increase in price, and rents tend to go up, driving higher income to the owners of the real estate.

REITs, companies that own or finance income-producing real estate, offer common shares to the public and are contingent on the state of the real estate market but trade on a public exchange and fluctuate in price like stocks. In the twenty-five-year period through December 31, 2017, public REITs have returned 10.75 percent annually. Interval funds give us exposure to private real estate. The National Council of Real Estate Investment Fiduciaries (NCREIF) Property Index, a private real estate composite, returned 9.17 percent over the same period and compares reasonably well to the S&P 500 Index, which returned 9.68 percent.

Most investors are familiar with publicly traded REITs, which are a sector of the stock market. Publicly traded REITs are highly correlated with stocks and with bonds. This high correlation makes publicly traded REITs less attractive for risk reduction through diversification. Publicly traded REITs can nonetheless be attractive investments at times, but keep in mind that you are buying a sector of the stock market, not a diversifying asset. Standards and Poor's has recently classified publicly traded REITs as a sector of the S&P 500, thus confirming my long-held assertion of this fact. I believe a reasonable expected return of private real estate mutual fund is around 6–8 percent net of fund and underlying manager fees. The bulk of this expected return is usually income.

TIMBERLAND

Timberland is a perfect investment because it can last more than a lifetime, and it can be regrown. Investing in timberland involves acquiring and managing forest assets for a financial return. Tree farms and managed natural forests are the two main subclasses. Timberland investments provide revenue from harvesting, leasing, and charging usage fees. They provide the potential for appreciation on both the value of the underlying land purchased as well as the value of the timber and timber growth on that land.

Based on the NCREIF Timberland Index, if someone invested $10,000 in 1987, that investment would have been worth $158,975 at the end of 2017.[7] Timberland is a smart investment that could be as profitable as stocks and more profitable than bonds. But the big advantage is, again, its low correlation, which makes it a great diversifier.

Considered an inflation hedge, timberland depends on wood-based products' ability to permeate multitudes of sectors across the global economy. US residential construction activity needs to move above long-term trend levels to reduce the backlog of housing demand. Less restrictive access to credit, increasing incomes, and improving employment rates will keep the housing demand trending higher.

Rising US consumption of building products will trigger investment in lumber and wood panel capacity in the US South, thus boosting the demand for regional timber. It will also offset the softer/more competitive China market for softwood log and lumber exports from US West. Coupled with a strong US dollar, it will create opportunities for Brazilian and Chilean producers of lumber and plywood and support their timber markets.

Institutional interest in core timberland markets in the United States and Australasia remains high. Market conditions require a disciplined acquisition approach. Another plus is the matter of taxes. When land is agriculturally zoned, it's valued for little other than the crops that are grown on it. Therefore, it is taxed at a highly-

---

7   "Versus Capital Real Estate (VCMIX) Real Assests (VCRRX)," VersusCapital, (Power-Point presentation, April 30, 2018.

reduced rate. Finally, whatever happens to the market, land is always there, and so is your investment—although the value may change and could result in losses.

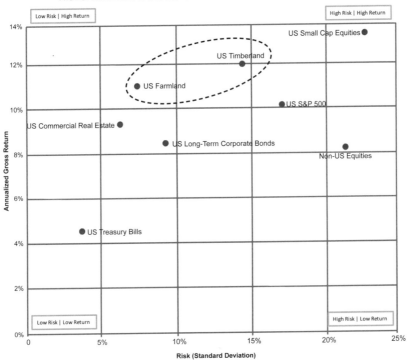

Asset Classes
HISTORICAL RETURN AND STANDARD DEVIATION (1972-2016)

SOURCE: VERSUS

Figure 4.2

FARMLAND

Real assets are direct investments in rural crop land assets producing food and fiber. The investment universe of farmland in the United States is valued at almost $2.7 trillion. Furthermore, the United States grows a diversity of crops, with a significant proportion of commodity crops originating in the Corn Belt, Mississippi Delta States, and Southern Plains.

The Pacific West, another important and diverse agricultural region, grows both annual and permanent cropland.

The two categories of these direct investments include the following:

- Row crop investments. These include annual crops such as corn, soybeans, cotton, wheat, and rice. These need to be replanted every year.

- Permanent crop investments. These include perennial crops such as fruits and nuts, which have both pre-production periods and mature periods. Permanent crops are perennials that do not need to be planted every year. Examples include almond and orange trees, as well as grape vineyards for both food and wine.

Investing in farmland means that you are not just investing in crops but in the productive capacity of the land base. Although returns will be based on the growth of those crops, they will also be based on the appreciation of land and other assets.

Increased productivity is one of the main contributors to economic growth in agriculture in the United States, and since 1970, productivity has doubled, while inputs have remained constant. Increased productivity contributes to, and supports, higher farmland values.

Sources of return for these assets vary. Leasing fees, land prices, and prices of underlying commodities are all included.

A February 2018 report from the United States Department of Agriculture's (USDA) Economic Research Service examining farmland values from 2000 to 2016 notes, "The value of farm real estate accounts for over 80% of the value of farm-sector assets and is an important indicator of the sector." The report, *Farmland Values, Land Ownership, and Returns to Farmland,* 2000–2016 (by Christopher Burns, Nigel Key, Sarah Tulman, Allison Borchers, and Jeremy Weber), states, "Economic theory suggests that farmland values will change in response to changes in the underlying factors that support them, namely, returns to farmland. One measure of returns to farmland is net cash farm income per acre, or the net return that an acre of farmland generates."[8]

Ultimately, the USDA report states, "Future trends in farmland values will depend on net cash returns to farmland, interest rates, and agricultural policy."

A period of high inflation and low (even negative) real interest rates encouraged leveraged acquisition of farmland in the late 1970s. Farmland has produced an 11.5 percent annualized return over the past twenty-six years, based on the NCREIF Farmland Index.[9]

Investment strategy focuses on portfolio investments targeting returns from leasing fees and land values and not the more volatile segments links to commodity pricing. These investments have shown historical returns with a positive correlation to inflation, a low or negative correlation to public equities and debt, low volatility, and stable income attributes.

James B. McCandless, managing director and Head of Global Real Estate at UBS, stated that "farmland has historically provided very attractive risk-adjusted returns, inflation protection, and good diversification for stock, bond, and real estate portfolios. Increasing

---

8   Christopher Burns, "Farmland Values, Land Ownership, and Returns to Farmland, 2000-2016," United States Department of Agriculture, Economic Research Report Number 245, February 2018, https://www.ers.usda.gov/webdocs/publications/87524/err-245.pdf?v=0.

9   "Versus Capital Real Estate (VCMIX) Real Assests (VCRRX)," VersusCapital.

global demand for farm commodities over the past few years has supported higher commodity prices, farm income, farmland rents, and farmland values. This dynamic has generated a period of excess returns on farmland. Global demand for farm commodities and the resulting excess returns farmland has been providing to investors have been slowed by the global recession and anemic, slow recovery."

ADVANTAGES OF REAL ASSETS

Real assets provide you with significant diversification benefits, as well as exposure to different stages of the economic cycle. Private real assets have generated attractive absolute and risk-adjusted returns relative to traditional stock and bond portfolios. The key benefits these asset classes have provided are high and stable cash flows and yield. Income streams are more predictable because continued demand for assets such as farmland (food) and real estate (housing and office space) is both stable and increasing. Many real asset investments have low volatility and thus can be long-term investments that free you from worrying about when to buy or sell. Their hard asset nature allows them to serve as a hedge against inflation.

> Private real assets have generated attractive absolute and risk-adjusted returns relative to traditional stock and bond portfolios.

They also allow you to gain exposure to international investing with limited currency risk. As economies develop globally and/or update infrastructure, demand for real assets continues to increase. Although many agriculture commodities markets are international, they are often priced in US currency.

Population growth will continue to affect real estate, infrastructure, farmland, and timberland—economic growth will also affect all four. Urbanization and construction will affect real estate, infrastructure, and timberland.

Arable land is that which is capable of being plowed and used to grow crops, and the world has lost one-third of its arable land in the past forty-plus years because of development, erosion, or pollution. This reduction will affect both farmland and timberland.

As I state at the beginning of this book, in the past, many investors have not been exposed to these diversifying assets. That is because they were not available to most investors. Now that they are, and now that knowledgeable professionals are able to guide investors as to their use, real assets are increasingly attractive to those seeking to diversify their portfolios.

DISADVANTAGES OF REAL ASSETS

Generally, each private real asset sector carries its own individual risks, but each asset class is ultimately subject to the effects of demand, supply, and capital market activity.

Real estate would be affected if GDP growth and job growth turn negative when an increasing supply of new buildings is available. As a result, rental rates could decline and lead to investors reducing the prices they are willing to pay for those assets.

Under private infrastructure, transportation, which includes airports, toll roads, and seaports, is more sensitive to economic growth. Utilities are more sensitive to regulatory changes, and communications is linked more to economic and technological change.

The greatest risk for farmland investing would be an extremely long and prolonged decline in crop prices. Crop prices are notoriously volatile and are affected by consumption, supply, and weather.

The 2018 USDA report (Burns et al.) states that net cash farm income fell from its 2013 peak in 2015 and 2016. "The primary factors driving lower net cash farm income are lower commodity prices and lower cash receipts," the report states. "As expectations for future net cash farm income have been adjusted downward, land value appreciation has moderated and even declined. The Northern Plains and Corn Belt, which had high levels of cropland value appreciation in 2009–14, had low to negative growth from 2015 to 2016, reflecting the drop in cash grain and oilseed prices."[10]

For private timberland, the biggest risk would be a sustained decline in the use of timber materials. This decline would be reflected in fewer homes and buildings being constructed, a drop in the use of paper and/or packaging, and/or a decline in biofuel usage. Amazon and other online retailers are a boon to the packaging industry, because every package sold and sent needs a box.

Another risk is the relative illiquidity of private real asset investments. Given the limited transaction activity and price discovery within these markets relative to public/listed asset investing, at times, exiting an investment takes longer than desired and occurs at a price that is different than one at which an investor would like to transact. Many of the real asset funds that I invest in are interval funds with limited liquidity that is in line with the limited liquidity of the underlying investments.

In researching this chapter, I have interviewed others who invest and work extensively in the area of real assets. One of the topics we discussed is the four key measurements of risk.

---

10   Ibid.

Historically, private real assets have experienced very low levels of risk in each of these categories:

- Standard deviation—Private real assets have had bond-like volatility.

- Correlation/beta—Private real assets have low correlation to traditional 60 percent equity and 40 percent bond portfolios.

- Max drawdown—Private real assets have had much lower drawdowns than traditional equities.

- Permanent impairment—Private real assets have enjoyed very low loss rates because of their hard asset nature.

For these reasons, real assets can be an effective tool for portfolio diversification.

Your Takeaway

- Real assets' benefits are equity-like returns with lower volatility and low correlation.

- Risks are primarily from deflationary economy and limited liquidity.

- These non-financial assets include real estate, infrastructure, agriculture property, and timberland.

- Real assets as part of a diversified portfolio allow you to minimize losses during equity market downturns and maintain exposure to market upside during bull markets.

- Because of their hard asset nature, real assets have enjoyed low maximum drawdowns historically and are good hedges against inflation.

CHAPTER 5

Alternative Lending: Connecting Outside the Bank

"Drive thy business or it will drive thee."

—Benjamin Franklin

AS WE EXPLORED IN EARLIER CHAPTERS, diversification is a proven way to spread your risk and decrease overall portfolio risk. Long-term investors have historically earned a premium over cash by putting their capital at risk. Alternative lending is another asset class to consider.

It's no secret that bank deposits earn very little these days, right around the 1 percent range. On the opposite side of the coin, if you were to open a credit card account and borrow money from the same bank that was paying you that 1 percent on your savings, what kind of interest would you pay them? Fifteen percent? Twenty percent? More? What's wrong with that? How can there be such a vast difference in what you earn from your own money and what the bank earns from its money?

Around 2007, entrepreneurs from the areas of financial services and technology looked into this issue and figured out that the ways banks provided credit to consumers and small businesses were inefficient and outdated. Enter the age of alternative lending or market place lending. Alternative online lending platforms have stepped into this market gap by connecting borrowers and lenders without needing to go through the bureaucracy often found at a bank.

ALTERNATIVE LENDING: A DEFINITION

The term *alternative lending* refers to lending that originated outside banks. At one time, that would have been a shocking concept. After all, banks have long enjoyed a traditional role in taking deposits from those with saving accounts and using these funds to loan out at significantly higher interest rates.

Instead of using savings account deposits to make loans, alternative lenders rely on technology to connect borrowers with investors in search of ways to earn interest. Once known as peer-to-peer lending, it is now known as *alternative lending* or *marketplace lending (MPL)*, and it is another excellent option for diversification.

Although this may sound new, channels outside traditional banks have always existed, often as small categories in the economy. But would you trust your personal data to the internet? Not everyone was sure consumers would take to that idea, and the comfort level wasn't immediate. However, banks themselves started offering consumers online accounts, and then the 2009 financial crisis arrived, with all its fallout and uncertainty.

After that, with traditional bank lending losing trust and favor, the growth of numerous online financial services accelerated. These lenders, which were previously relatively inconsequential to the overall lending experience, are now a significant presence in the market. Why? Because with alternative lenders, borrowers have the following:

- A more competitive interest rate—This is especially true considering the rates most borrowers are currently paying.

- A better application experience—Time is money to these borrowers, and the convenience of the internet is a big improvement over traditional ways they may have applied for loans in the past.

While borrowers like the ease of these loans, investors are attracted to alternative lenders because of the potential for higher yields in a protracted low-interest-rate environment. Furthermore, many borrowers—who are now used to contacting various types of transactions online—are attracted to the ease of using the internet.

WHO ARE THESE ALTERNATIVE LENDERS?

Lending Club was the first, as many investors are already aware. A peer-to-peer lending company headquartered in San Francisco, Lending Club offers investors an opportunity to purchase notes corresponding to different loans, grades, and terms. Investors then receive monthly principal and interest payments as borrowers pay off their three- or five-year debt consolidation loans serviced by Lending Club.

Social Finance, Inc. (SoFi) offers student loan and medical resident refinancing, among others. Prosper, another lender, offers loans for debt consolidation, home improvement, auto and vehicle, baby and adoption, small business, and special occasion.

As of this writing in 2018, of the estimated $100 billion loans outstanding, the alternative lending market is still small relative to the multi-trillion-dollar market for consumer and small business credit at traditional banks.

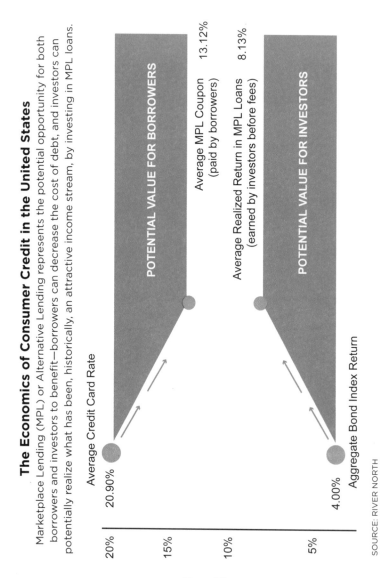

The Economics of Consumer Credit in the United States

Marketplace Lending (MPL) or Alternative Lending represents the potential opportunity for both borrowers and investors to benefit—borrowers can decrease the cost of debt, and investors can potentially realize what has been, historically, an attractive income stream, by investing in MPL loans.

POTENTIAL VALUE FOR BORROWERS

Average Credit Card Rate

20.90%

Average MPL Coupon (paid by borrowers) 13.12%

Average Realized Return in MPL Loans (earned by investors before fees) 8.13%

POTENTIAL VALUE FOR INVESTORS

Aggregate Bond Index Return

4.00%

20%

15%

10%

5%

Figure 5.1

HOW DOES IT WORK?

Working with alternative lenders doesn't differ that much from working with banks. The lenders work with borrowers to originate the loan. They perform underwriting to measure the borrower's credit, and they service the loan. That includes collecting principal and interest on behalf of the lender or investor throughout the life of the loan.

HIGH-TECH AVENUES OFFER SAVINGS ON BOTH SIDES

Banks have branches. They pay salaries, rent, utilities, and other costs before they open those branches on any given day. Alternative lenders haven't been around long enough to become laden with those costs. Because they have no brick-and-mortar branches, they rely on what they know best—technology. Using state-of-the-art technology can lead to lower operating costs and other advantages that traditional banks cannot match.

These savings result in lower interest rates for borrowers and higher yields for investors. Furthermore—and you may well relate to this—the days of wanting to visit a bank and talk to your banker have passed. Most customers/borrowers now think of themselves as *users*, and they prepare to engage online, especially when looking for a loan. A borrower generally sets up automatic payment on MPL loans so they don't need to log in to make a payment and certainly don't have to write a check. According to a 2017 Transunion study of more than 2 million borrowers, people prioritized the repayment of these types of installment loans over credit cards, auto loans, and even their mortgages.[11] Most alternative lending platforms take automatic payments directly out of the consumer's checking account. This is another win-win situation for both borrower and lender.

---

11   "Consumers Place Personal Loans Atop the Credit Mountain," TransUnion, May 17, 2017, https://newsroom.transunion.com/consumers-place-personal-loans-atop-the-credit-mountain/.

Business Model Driving Lower Costs

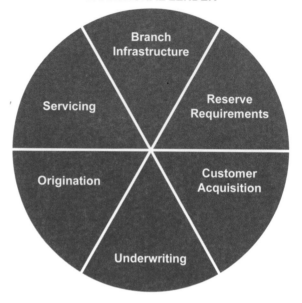

TRADITIONAL LENDER

ALTERNATIVE LENDER

SOURCE: LENDING CLUB

Figure 5.2

TYPES OF ALTERNATIVE LENDING

Various types of borrowers are attracted to the alternative lending industry.

Consumer

The typical alternative lending portfolio includes primarily consumer loans. These loans are generally relatively small, averaging approximately $12-15,000 per loan. These loans are made as short-duration instruments and are self-amortizing, meaning that part of the principal is paid back with every monthly payment, so generally, their duration is about one and one-half years.

Also in 2017, Harris Poll surveyed more than two thousand US adults on behalf of Northwestern Mutual. They found that 40 percent of those with debt were spending up to half their monthly income paying back that debt.[12] Considering that credit cards lack a set schedule of repayment, that their interest rates are usually variable, and that those rates can increase if a borrower misses a payment, alternative lending is especially attractive. Borrowers have a set schedule of payments, so they can repay both principal and interest over a set time span, usually about three to five years. The loan processor often debits the payment from the consumer borrower's checking account.

The consumer borrower generally takes these loans generally to consolidate other, more expensive loans that he or she may have outstanding, such as credit card debt loans that may charge interest of 20 percent to 28 percent per annum. The direct-to-consumer loans on lending platforms vary the rate considerably depending on several factors, including duration of the loan and credit quality of

---

12 "40% of Americans spend up to half of their income servicing debt," MarketWatch, April 30, 2017, https://www.marketwatch.com/story/40-of-americans-spend-half-of-their-income-servicing-debt-2017-04-27.

the borrower. On average, the loans are made to the consumer at a gross rate of around 14 percent. So, if the rate that the consumer has agreed to pay on the loan is less than he or she was paying before, that borrower is happy.

Small Business

Alternative lending is especially attractive to small businesses, for a number of reasons. As we've already explored here, that lack of credit availability after the 2009 financial crisis slowed the movement of capital to small businesses. Between 2007 and 2012, the number of loans under $1 million made by the traditional banking system markedly decreased.

Applying to a bank can be a lengthy process, and months can pass before the borrower has funds in hand. For a small business, this can make the difference between disaster and survival. Alternative lenders can qualify borrowers in minutes, if not seconds, and they can often deliver in a matter of days.

Alternative lenders are often backed by venture capital firms. These include Union Square Ventures, Google Ventures, and Index Ventures. OnDeck Capital has raised more than $300 million from top-tier investors, and that is just one example. Lending Club obtained financing from the public markets and is a publicly traded company. Goldman Sachs recently launched a direct consumer lending platform called Marcus. Many of the large banks actually buy whole loans from the lending platforms, because internet lending platforms are often more efficient than banks in underwriting smaller consumer loans.

NOT AS STRINGENT

Alternative lenders aren't as stringent as traditional lenders regarding creditworthiness. Businesses with mediocre or even poor credit are still able to get loans. This doesn't mean the alternative lenders are intentionally more careless than banks. They consider themselves to be more innovative by considering factors other than the credit rating of a business. Some of these considerations are shipping schedules, education level of the borrower, and social network connections. The approach is one of flexibility with an eye on the changes in the way small businesses operate today. The jury is still out on whether these other pieces of information will help reduce bad debt expense. The risk is that in the next consumer recession, these supposed innovations will prove to be a mirage.

These lenders are able to compete with banks because they do not have to deal with the same regulatory requirements, capital needs, and restrictions. As a result, they enjoy more flexibility and can experiment in ways most banks cannot.

VARIOUS CAPITAL NEEDS

Alternative lenders are able to offer capital for many different types of needs. Borrowers can get equipment loans, term loans, factoring (where a business can get back 80 percent of its outstanding invoices), and merchant cash advances (a percentage of sales paid back daily or weekly).

HELP FOR FRANCHISEES

Franchisees are another growing segment of the alternative lending market. To finance a franchise, a borrower usually has three choices—a traditional bank, a small business loan, or a loan with an alternative lender. Although the Small Business Administration guarantees loans issued by banks and offers competitive interest rates, it has many hindrances similar to those of traditional banks. Borrowers must provide collateral and personal guarantees, and they must fill out a lengthy loan application that asks for personal and business financial histories, income tax returns, resumes, and profit and loss statements. This application is not available online, either; it must be submitted on paper. Furthermore, once the borrower submits that application, a traditional bank must approve it.

Someone preparing to buy a first franchise or to expand or upgrade current franchises is already aware of the importance of time management. To this person, finding and securing a loan are simply tasks to be added to a number of other functions one can complete online without leaving the place of business or spending hours on paperwork.

More and more, this time-pressed franchisee will turn to a company like ApplePie Capital, an alternative lender specializing in financing franchises and offering to lend to qualified franchisees. In addition to loans for unit purchasing, the firm offers refinancing, equipment financing, and recapitalizations for those who self-funded their franchise business and want to borrow against it to free up capital.

International

OnDeck, Kabbage, and SoFi are among the lenders venturing into the international market. The total transaction value in the alternative financing segment amounted to $20.5 billion in 2017. According to Statista, the total transaction value is expected to show an annual growth rate (CAGR 2018-2022) of 29 percent, resulting in a total of

$56.8 billion by 2022.[13] The highest cumulated transaction value in 2017 ($9.8 billion) was in China.

Challenges in the international market, such as regulations, the necessary increased time commitment, and the problems involved in creating products that must fit the culture and needs of a particular market, cause some to hesitate, however. Still, statistics indicate that the international market is an investment that offers excellent potential along with these risks.

What Does the Future Hold?

Not everyone agrees on the future of alternative lending, and some go as far as warning that it is a bubble. Chris Myers warned in *Forbes* on June 22, 2016, that "plentiful capital and sky-high valuations created a bubble that only a handful of the most forward-thinking players will survive."[14] He points to the fact that these loans are created to help borrowers pay off credit card debt. Although the loans are used for that purpose, many borrowers continue to use their credit cards, thus owing not only the alternative loan but also the newly created credit card debt.

Myers also addresses the problem of *stacking*, which occurs when a borrower takes out loans from several unsuspecting lenders around the same time. This increases the borrower's default risk substantially, and because of lagging data-reporting functions, alternative lenders are not informed in time to stop the stacking.

---

13   "Alternative Financing," Statista, https://www.statista.com/outlook/297/100/alternative-financing/worldwide.

14   Chris Myers, "The Alternative Lending Bubble Is Here, And It's Time To Do Something About It," *Forbes*, June 22, 2016, https://www.forbes.com/sites/chrismyers/2016/06/22/the-alternative-lending-bubble-is-here-and-its-time-to-do-something-about-it/#3c22304611b3.

Myers describes the cycle as "an adverse selection problem in which the worst debt offenders are most attracted to the industry's refinancing options, which puts the entire model severely at risk when we go into a typical economic downswing."

While alternative lending is not low risk, I do believe that it will prove itself to be lower risk than junk (high yield) bond funds in the next recession. Only time will tell.

DIVERSIFICATION OPPORTUNITY

In writing this book, I interviewed Philip K. Bartow, portfolio manager at RiverNorth. He believes that investors should consider adding alternative lending asset exposure within the short-duration, credit-sensitive portion of their portfolios, given the broad and continued tightening of corporate credit.

"From our perspective, adding this asset class to one's portfolio has offered the potential for higher returns and lower volatility versus a portfolio that consisted of solely liquid fixed income products, while diversifying away from large corporate, bullet pay securities within one's allocation to credit-sensitive assets," Bartow said.

On one side of the equation, we have consumers and small business people who want to restructure their loans. On the other side, alternative lending platforms match investors with borrowers for a small transaction and processing fee. This allows both investors and borrowers to get a better rate of return than they would achieve via a typical bank or credit card loan.

The whole loan market has been around for some time and was relatively common in the 1980s, and to some extent it was a precursor to alternative lending. The alternative lending market attracted high net-worth and institutional investors to the platforms in 2011, and by 2014, some limited partnerships were specifically investing in loans from alternative lending platforms. The first MPL interval mutual fund came out in June 2016. Prior to digital platforms, banks were buying whole consumer loans from local banks, aggregating the loans, and selling them to third-party insurance companies. However, those were bigger loans, not the consumer loans that are so prevalent today.

Focusing on credit scores between 600 and 750, alternative lending platforms originate whole loans with an average of around $12-15,000 each. These loans are placed on the reselling part of their platform, where buyers such as institutions, banks, alternative lending funds, partnerships, and individual investors can review, evaluate, and buy. As an example, Lending Club originates and then posts loans on the company website for investors. You can go to Lending Club or other alternative platforms and look at both sides of these transactions. As mentioned before, most borrowers have automatic deductions coming out of their checking account.

Bad Debts and Expenses

Although gross yield on one of these loans is about 13 percent to 14 percent, unfortunately, there are extensive bad debt expenses that generally run between 4 percent and 6 percent in normal economic environments and spike higher when the economy goes into a recession. In addition to that, there are loan processing expenses (approximately 0.55 percent) for the custody and collection, which the consumer pays to the loan processor. Sometimes loan origination fees knock down the net rate to investors, as well. Add to that general expenses (0.50 percent or higher) by a fund company, along with a fund company's asset management fee (0.95 percent or higher), and in total, expenses can push the net expected return of alternative lending funds down to approximately 6 percent or 7 percent.

Should You Buy Directly?

The primary risk for alternative lending is credit quality specifically, which needs to be watched very closely. If bad debt expenses should go to 11 percent, we would expect alternative lending to become a break-even investment. If we should experience a surge in unemployment and a drop in income for the general population, that will cause a surge of bad debt expense and potentially wipe out any income stream from the portfolio. In a severe, bad debt environment, the investor could lose money.

For now, however, alternative lending investing makes sense, in my opinion, for diversification because of its extremely short duration and above-average yield. Philip K. Bartow says it well: "There is no free lunch in the current fixed income markets with the Federal Reserve moving front-end rates higher; investors crave income, but would prefer to not take on duration risk in their fixed income portfolios. Alternative lending can potentially offer an interesting solution: shorter duration with a high level of current income."

─────────── **Your Takeaway** ───────────

- Alternative lending is lending that is originated outside banks.

- More and more often, time-pressed consumers, small business owners, and franchisees will turn to alternative lenders, because they appreciate the flexibility and ease of the application process and because they will, as a rule, receive funds sooner than they would with a bank.

- Investors are attracted to alternative lenders because of the potential for higher yields in a protracted low-interest-rate environment.

- Alternative lending investing makes sense for diversification because of its extremely short duration and above-average yield.

CHAPTER 6

Variance Risk Premium Harvesting

"Time is money."

—BENJAMIN FRANKLIN

THE EASIEST WAY TO UNDERSTAND variance risk premium (VRP) harvesting is to think of it as selling financial insurance. We insure our cars. We insure our homes. We insure our health and our lives. The primary reason people buy insurance is to guard against financial disaster. In return for taking on these risks, insurance companies charge a price they believe will allow them to make money. Thus, the premiums consumers pay are expected to outweigh the payouts on the policies.

According to Karan Sood, portfolio manager at Cboe Vest, "When it comes to personal property insurance, the cost of protection to the insured, over time, is usually greater than the expected loss. Buyers may recognize this, but are compelled by fear, risk-aversion or regulatory reasons to buy this protection. The personal property insurance industry is arguably characterized by an imbalance between excessive demand and limited supply. This asymmetry may lead to a higher price for insurance than the price the probability-weighted expected loss calculation may suggest. Put another way, the potential asymmetry means the probability and magnitude of expected losses implied from the price of insurance may be higher than the frequency and magnitude of losses observed in reality."

Investment insurance in the financial markets may work in a similar manner; numerous buyers seek protection against adverse market price changes, while potentially few are prepared to sell it. The demand for insurance against adverse market changes is generally expressed as demand for options on equity indexes, such as the S&P 500 Index. The potential asymmetry between buyers and sellers of options affects their prices to the extent that the probability and magnitude of index returns implied by the prices is different from the frequency and magnitude of returns observed in reality.

VRP is the premium someone is willing to pay to hedge against variation in future realized volatilities or price changes. In short, it is a risk-transfer service in the financial market. It is similar to selling traditional insurance, because you are taking on risk in exchange for the premium. In most periods, sellers of options will collect premiums with modest to minimal losses or payouts. In some market scenarios, sellers will have to pay the buyer of those options more than you sold them for, thus creating a loss.

OPTION WRITING

Option strategies have been a part of the investment landscape for five decades. They are a type of derivative security, meaning that their value derives from the value of an underlying investment. Some conservative strategies are meant to hedge investment exposures or generate income, while others can be highly speculative.

Collateralized put writing and *covered call writing* are the two of the most common strategies involving options. That is not to say these strategies cannot lose money but rather that, when applied to underlying stocks or stock indices, they have historically generated equity-like returns with lower volatility. Option contracts can be bought or sold on individual securities, indices, or numerous other asset classes. Built around standardized benchmarks, portfolios can be transparent, liquid, unleveraged, and cost-effective.

IMPORTANT TERMINOLOGY

Let's start by defining some terms.

Underlying

The security, index, or other asset upon which an option contract is written.

Call Option

A call option is an agreement that allows the purchaser to buy a specified number of shares of the underlying security at a future date (expiration) and at a specified price (strike price) up until and including the expiration date in exchange for a payment or premium.

Put Option

A put option is an agreement that allows the purchaser to sell a specified number of shares of the underlying security at a future date (expiration) and at a specified price (strike price) up until and including the expiration date in exchange for a payment or premium.

Strike Price

The agreed-upon price at which an option may be exercised, bought for a call, or sold for a put.

Option Contract Size

One option contract typically gives the purchaser the right to buy 100 shares of a security. For example, if you purchased ten option contracts, you would be able to purchase up to 1,000 shares of that security at the strike price.

Expiration Date

The expiration date is the date when the option contract ends; that is, it can no longer be exercised after that date._

Premium

This is the amount of money the option seller receives from the option buyer; the price of the option.

In the Money

The security or index is trading at a level that would make it worthwhile for the owner of the option to exercise it. For a call option, this means the underlying security or index is above the strike price. For a put option, this means the security or index is below the strike price.

Out of the Money

The security or index is trading at a level where it would not make sense for the option owner to exercise it. For a call option, this means that the current price or index level is below the strike price. For a put option, this means the current price or index level is above the strike price.

At the Money

The underlying security is trading at the option strike price.

Implied Volatility

Implied volatility is the level of volatility reflected in current option prices. This can be thought of as the market's "forecast" of what the volatility will be over a future period.

Realized Volatility

Realized volatility is the actual volatility that was experienced by a security or index over a period of time.

Option Premium Time Decay

Options tend to trend downward toward zero over time. Writing (selling) options allows the option writer to benefit from the natural decline in value of options due to time decay as they get closer to expiration date. Option premiums (prices) tend to decay faster as they get closer to expiration.

Option Time Decay

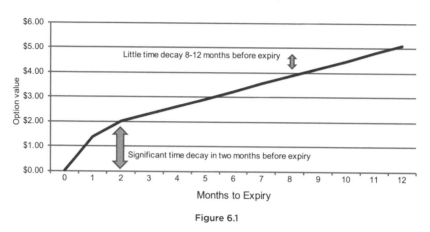

Figure 6.1

POSITIVE EXPECTED RETURN

A natural return is built in this market in that the option prices (premiums that determine implied volatility) generate a return in excess of the losses generated by the actual volatility. To clarify the implied volatility concept, price or premium of an option along with its strike price, expiration date and current underlying security are used to calculate implied volatility. Therefore, an investor who is selling premium (options) gets to keep that difference over time, so it has a positive natural expected return. It is going to vary over time, it is not linear, and it will result in periods of losses. *Expected return* is a statistical term and not a prediction or forecast. Assets with positive expected returns will at times experience losses.

HOW PUT WRITING WORKS

The seller (or writer) of a put gives the buyer the right to sell the underlying index or security at a specified strike price up to and on the expiration date, receiving a premium (payment) in exchange for assuming market risk.

If the underlying security's market price falls below the strike price, it is "in the money," and the put owner could exercise the option contract against the seller. If it remains above the strike price, it is "out of the money," and unless the price of the underlying index or security changes, the option will eventually expire, worthless. As you can see, basically, the strike price

The strike price minus the premium collected gives you the break-even number.

minus the premium collected gives you the break-even number at which the option seller would start to lose money on the put-write.

Short Put Payoff Diagram

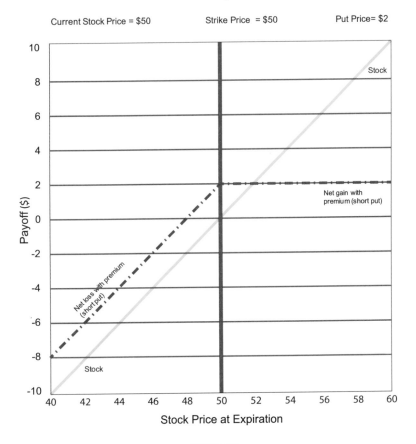

Figure 6.2

Let's examine this in insurance terms again. If you are the seller, you sell insurance that the underlying is not going to fall below a certain level or price. If the underlying's price stays the same, you keep the whole premium. If it goes down a little bit, you end up paying back some of the premium to the buyer of the option. And if it goes down a lot, you end up paying more back to the buyer than you received for the premium on the option, thus creating a loss on that option write position.

Collateralized Put Option Writing

This is a strategy in which the account selling puts has sufficient collateral (cash or Treasury bills or notes are common collateral) in the event that the put options sold are exercised against the put seller. In this case, the put seller has liquid assets available that can be used to close out (buy back) the options contract or purchase the security at the agreed-upon strike price. This strategy provides long market exposure (beta) with some downside cushion provided by the premium collected.

Index Put Writing at the Systematic Level

One passive index put writing strategy would be to simply sell a one-month, "at-the-money" (where the market price is equal to the strike price) put option on the S&P 500 Index, fully collateralized by short-term Treasuries. After a month, when the option expires, the portfolio would just sell a new option with a strike price at the prevailing level of the index.

The process is then repeated monthly. To put it simply, the put option seller collects option premiums twelve times per year, settles any options that expire in the money, and receives income from investments held as collateral. This approach is meant to capture and compound the collected option premiums and collateral income to generate an equity-like total return while mitigating or toning down equity and volatility risk.

The average gross put option premium has been over 1.5 percent per month for the last thirty years, or roughly 18 percent per annum. The actual returns of this passive strategy would be lower, because the premiums collected are partially offset by transaction costs and by the cost incurred in cases where puts expire in the money and the contracts are exercised by their buyers. Some of the options written will result in losses. I expect this strategy to provide equity-like returns over long periods of time but to have substantial short-term variation from the market.

EQUITY INDEX PUT WRITING'S ROLE IN PORTFOLIOS

Some investors use put writing as an equity substitute, pursuing equity-like returns over the long term with less volatility than the broader equity markets. Others find the historically less volatile return profile, particularly around periods of market turmoil, to be a suitable complement or replacement for certain pricier and less liquid alternative investment strategies typically used to mitigate portfolio risk.

Finally, index put writing produces some income but has higher risk than bonds over time—more like equity risk. It nonetheless could be appealing to some investors who have been prompted by low bond yields to allocate away from fixed income but are still wary of adding to their traditional equity holdings and need a little more income than stocks can provide. Put writing as an equity substitute has some advantages but is less tax efficient than owning equities outright.

BENEFITS OF EQUITY INDEX PUT WRITING

The addition of collateralized put writing strategies can benefit investors' portfolios as they seek to smooth volatility and manage equity risk. For example, some index put writing vehicles are available as active strategies that seek to enhance returns in various ways. Active strategies may alter the collateral used, sell options with somewhat different maturities, or seek to capitalize on better execution in closing out option positions and initiating new ones (rolling of option contracts) each month. Such active approaches may provide a more effective way to capture the attractive, risk-adjusted return potential of index put writing.

EQUITY INDEX PUT WRITING IN THE CURRENT ENVIRONMENT

Index put writing can provide a way to seek equity exposure while mitigating risk, especially when used as an additional diversifier. I generally recommend that clients have most of their equity exposure in regular stocks but have a small portion in these equity VRP harvesting strategies if they need more income. In times of market turbulence, put writers can benefit from the collection of premiums paid by put buyers who aim to mitigate short-term losses. During volatile markets, the premiums can increase, as investors often "overpay" for risk mitigation. However, moves from low volatility or implied volatility to high implied volatility will often result in losses, as the prices for puts go up and exceed the price at which the put was sold. Periods of increasing volatility are also often accompanied by price declines, moving puts into the money and resulting in realized losses when index price is below strike price.

A rise in interest rates could benefit a put writing strategy, as its short-duration collateral investments will usually generate a higher yield as interest rates rise. The return/risk history of index put writing offers a compelling choice, especially at this time, when investors are looking for effective solutions to difficult portfolio challenges.

EQUITY VRP CAPTURE

Equity index put writing is a form of equity VRP capture. Although this put writing strategy provides some equity exposure and VRP exposure, it generally has about a two-thirds or half of the beta of the stock market. This equity VRP capture exposure gives you both equity and VRP capture.

For example, a collateralized index put writer collateralizes positions with short-term Treasury holdings or similar high-quality fixed-income securities. For this put writer, the long-term goal is for the premiums received from selling index put options, minus the losses on negative positions, combined with the income from the collateral portfolio, generate an equity-like return with less volatility than the underlying equity index. Index put writing strategies take such individual periodic, like monthly, transactions and seek to systematize and repeat them over time for the benefit of a fund's investors.

COVERED CALL WRITING STRATEGIES

The most popular form of equity VRP strategies is *covered call writing strategies*. A covered call strategy has a similar expected risk return profile as a collateralized put writing strategy. This equivalency is called *put-call parity*. Put-call parity is essentially a formula that shows there are two ways to implement equity VRP strategies.

Stock – Call = Cash – Put

Stock = stock price or the current market value of the underlying

Call = price of the call option; the call premium

Cash = the present value of the strike price (x), discounted from the value on the expiration date at the risk-free rate

Put = price of the put; the put premium

Covered call strategies and collateralized put writing strategies have similar payoff profiles, as shown on the respective payoff diagrams above and below. A covered call strategy buys a stock (or underlying) and writes (sells) a call.

Covered Call Payoff Diagram

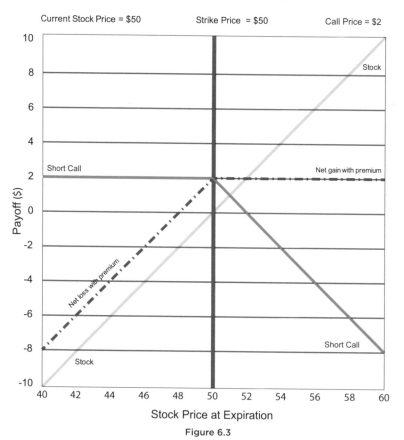

Figure 6.3

It is mathematically equivalent to cash minus put, which is a cash collateralized put writing strategy. Put-call parity illustrates why this works. Both are types of equity VRP. The volatility on the covered call strategy is lower than the volatility for an index like the S&P 500. The benefits for the investor include additional income and lower portfolio volatility. Thus, you have equity-like expected returns with lower expected risk and higher expected yield. The covered call expected return stream is illustrated below as the call portion of the strategy converts some expected price appreciation from a long only strategy into a call write option premium within the covered call strategy.

Expected Return Stream
PRICE APPRECIATION, DIVIDEND, AND OPTION PREMIUM

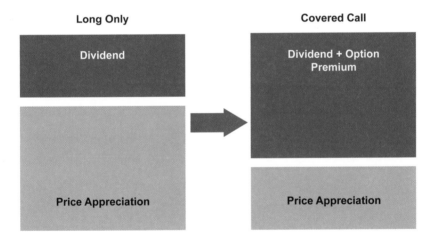

Figure 6.4

Covered call and collateralized put writing on individual stocks or equity indices comprise a small niche of the option-based strategies but are the most well-known. Many different asset classes exist—not just the US stock market, far from it—and many of these other asset classes have options available to trade. In addition to equity options, investors will find options with underlying asset classes including energy, foreign exchange, agricultural commodities, livestock, interest rates, metals, credit, and even options on options.

> In addition to equity options, investors will find options with underlying asset classes including energy, foreign exchange, agricultural commodities, livestock, interest rates, metals, credit, and even options on options.

VRP is the premium option buyers pay to sellers. Again, it is similar to the cost of buying insurance.

Option Writing on Both Sides

There are some option selling strategies that offer options on both sides of the trade. As a result, they will sell options and collect premiums from buyers who believe the underlying's price will be going up a lot or need to hedge their business or portfolio to offset this risk. They will also sell options and collect premiums from buyers who are hedging against or speculating on the underlying's price going down a lot. Most option buyers across all markets are doing hedging transactions; these buyers, such as those of commodities-based options, have strategic reasons for their purchases.

For example, farmers need to protect against falling agriculture prices. Food packagers need to protect against a surge in prices. Exporting, importing, and overseas businesses need to protect against a falling or rising dollar. Airlines have huge negative exposure to rising jet fuel prices and need to protect against a sharp rise in fuel costs by buying calls. On the other hand, energy producers could be wiped out if oil prices drop, so they hedge themselves with the purchase of puts. So, as you can see, there are two sides to every risk.

Option sellers who offer options on both sides can thus collect both sides of the premium stream. One is generally going to be a winner, and one is going to be a loser, unless the underlying's price does not change. This generally creates a positive return for the option sellers, because they have also captured the difference between implied and realized volatility, which has been positive over time, resulting in a persistent positive expected return. If the prices change a lot, however, the losses on the losing option could be larger than the gain on the winning position, resulting in a net loss for the combined put and call write position at that time.

Volatilities for different asset classes do not tend to move in unison. Although there is some correlation between different asset classes, stock market volatility is not highly correlated to the volatility of asset classes such as commodities or currencies.

There are funds available that harvest volatility across multiple asset classes. By harvesting volatility premiums across diverse asset classes, you are exposed to asset class volatilities that are uncorrelated or have low correlations. You have further diversification based on which specific asset within an asset class the options are written.

> Although there is some correlation between different asset classes, stock market volatility is not highly correlated to the volatility of asset classes such as commodities or currencies.

As mentioned earlier in this section, if the fuel prices were to rise dramatically, an airline's profits could be wiped out, so they buy fuel hedges to transfer this risk and allow them to purchase a certain amount of fuel at a locked-in price. On the other side, energy producers can be wiped out if prices decline substantially. Therefore, they can buy puts to lock in the price at which they can sell some of their production. There is a tremendous opportunity to sell options to the producers or users of commodities—airlines on one side of the example, energy producers on the other. For obvious reasons, both sides want to hedge large price movements that could hurt their profitability. One wants to hedge against price increases, while the other wants to hedge against price decreases. Their differing needs and risks help make it possible to harvest premiums from both sides of the same underlying commodity.

Short Put and Call

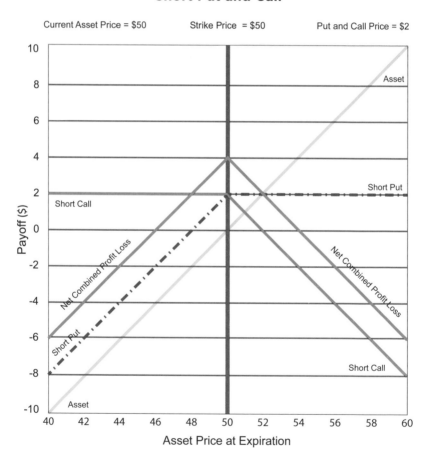

Figure 6.5

Hedges are not only used by airlines. Indeed, the use of hedges is widespread across diverse industries, because hedges reduce a risk that many businesses cannot afford to take. But again, each side of the coin has its own risks. A cattle farmer may hedge against a drop in livestock prices, while a meat processor would hedge against rising prices. Whether it's an auto manufacturer who has hedged the price of aluminum, an importer who wants to hedge the price of currency, or a soy bean farmer hedging against lower crop prices, there's always another side wanting to hedge the opposite outcome.

Selling options on both sides gives you exposure to both volatility premiums (as opposed to primarily directional bets and asset class returns). If the market stays basically flat, this strategy would make money by collecting premiums over time in excess of the costs for settling positions that finished in the money.

This is partially due to the historical spread, or difference, between implied and realized volatility. Implied volatility is the level of volatility reflected in current option prices. This can be thought of as a cost of insuring against adverse price moves in a future period. On the other hand, realized volatility is simply the actual volatility that was experienced by a security or index over a period of time. This is the historical level of volatility for a certain period of time.

Option buyers tend to overpay for volatility exposure or protection. This has led to implied volatilities typically being higher than realized volatilities over time. Therefore, an investor who is selling options gets to keep that difference over time, so it has a positive natural return. It will vary over time, it is not linear, and it will result in periods of losses.

What we've just covered is difficult to understand for most because it uses unfamiliar terms, and it's not something discussed as frequently as other investments. The most important thing to remember and to discuss with your adviser is the attractiveness of using these for diversification. With everything from reinsurance and real estate to timberland, the benefit derives from how they fit into— and help reduce risk in—the portfolio. That's where your financial adviser comes in. I am not advocating that you try to implement these strategies on your own. VRP harvesting is available in mutual funds and interval funds. VRP harvesting, when executed within a mutual fund or interval, has an additional execution risk. Specifically, there is a risk that a fund manager strays from risk controls or specific mandates. This happens with stock mutual funds as well, but the magnitude and speed of the risk is potentially amplified with VRP strategies if risk mandates are not steadfastly adhered to by a fund manager. If you are a savvy stock market operator who likes looking at his or her portfolio every day, a self-managed covered call strategy could make some sense, but only after you thoroughly study the subject and test your abilities in real time before committing any real money. Time, discipline, and management are required even with the most conservative of the VRP strategies, including covered call writing strategies.

Again, consider the analogy with which we started this discussion. If you start thinking in terms of insurance and risk transfer, it is not that much different than if you were an insurance company selling insurance on financial instruments. In a nutshell, that's what is happening, and as an investor, that's where you're investing your money.

Karan Sood summarizes as follows: "In the current low interest rate environment, many investors are looking for alternatives to fixed coupon bonds to meet their income requirements. A way to do this is to take advantage of the potential asymmetry in the demand for insurance against equity market volatility, expressed as demand for options on equity indexes such as the S&P 500 Index. Since there are generally more buyers of these options than there are sellers, the prices of options tend to reflect a wider range of expected returns (higher volatility) than that which is observed in reality."

Your Takeaway

- The insurance industry was founded upon the idea of risk transfer.

- VRP is the premium someone is willing to pay to hedge against variation in future realized volatilities or price changes.

- Volatility levels for different asset classes typically do not move in unison.

- Hedgers buy options to reduce their business or portfolio risk. Different hedgers may need to hedge price changes in opposite directions, thus making it possible to harvest premiums of both sides of the same commodity.

- The key driver—as is always the case with diversification—is how these investments fit into and help reduce overall risk in your portfolio.

CHAPTER 7

Add Diversifying Assets; Reduce Your Risk

"Well done is better than well said."

—BENJAMIN FRANKLIN

WISER DIVERSIFICATION REQUIRES the use of asset classes that have low correlation with stocks and, preferably, between each other. Including low-correlation or uncorrelated assets that can maintain their low correlations in down equity markets is essential for building a less volatile and safer portfolio. This chapter is a more detailed quantitative discussion of the content in Chapter 2. As we showed earlier, adding uncorrelated assets to a portfolio reduces risk. The example below shows risk reduction in the idealized hypothetical case of adding assets with zero correlation.

Portfolio Risk Reduction from Adding Assets with Zero Correlation

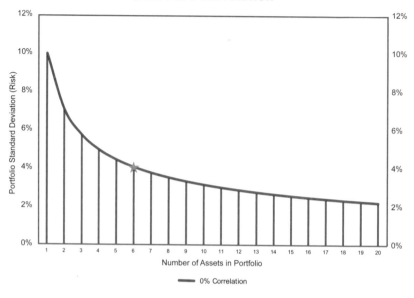

Figure 7.1

The key is having assets that have low correlations or are uncorrelated. This does not mean that each asset is low risk; it means that the overall risk is reduced as a result of the diversification. The graph shows how risk decreases as uncorrelated assets are added to the portfolio. At six uncorrelated assets, risk is down almost 60 percent. In this simplified example, each asset has an expected volatility of 10 percent. For simplicity, let's assume that each asset had an expected return of 7 percent. If you own one of the assets, you have a 7 percent expected return with a 10 percent risk (expected volatility). However, as you add assets with 7 percent expected returns, 10 percent risk, and no correlation, your return remains the same (7 percent, in this example), but risk falls with each additional asset. It falls quickly with the second asset and more slowly as the numbers grow. I highlighted six assets, because that number achieves the bulk of your risk reduction. The magic of diversification is that your expected return remains the same, 7 percent, *even though your risk is down almost 60 percent.* Diversification is your only free lunch: your expected return remaining high while your risk decreases.

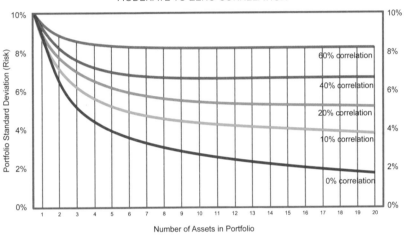

The Holy Grail

PORTFOLIO RISK REDUCTION FROM ADDING ASSETS OF
MODERATE TO ZERO CORRELATION

SOURCE: *PRINCIPLES* BY RAY DALIO, PG. 56-57

Figure 7.2

Risk reduction is not only important to helping you weather storms and sleep better at night; it is also a way to help your compounded returns compound faster. To visualize this concept, Figure 7.3 shows the dollar loss, gain, and net loss of four separate initial $1,000 investments, each with an average return of 0 percent and each experiencing one year down and then year up with percentage changes of equal magnitude. These four different volatilities result in dramatically different ending values. The less risky (lower volatility) portfolio has better end results than the higher-risk portfolio even though the average return is identical (0 percent). This is a simplified example, but it shows that outcomes are dependent on risk, not just average return.

Values Changes of a $1,000 Portfolio with 0% Average Returns

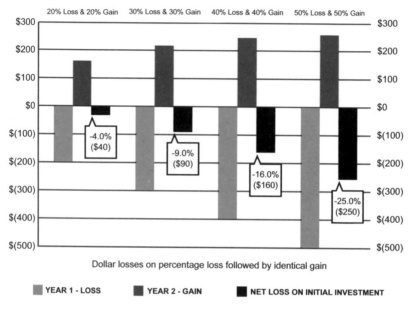

Dollar losses on percentage loss followed by identical gain

■ YEAR 1 - LOSS   ■ YEAR 2 - GAIN   ■ NET LOSS ON INITIAL INVESTMENT

Figure 7.3

Over this short, two-year period, the volatility drag on the portfolio is readily apparent when the volatility differences are large. In the real world, the expected volatility of diversified portfolios versus stock/bond-only balanced portfolios is less extreme, but the time periods are measured in decades. The volatility drag is significant as it compounds, even if it is small over a two-year time span. You can see the big difference in average return and compounded return at different levels of portfolio volatility over twenty years in Figure 7.4. The higher-risk all stock portfolio has a larger volatility drag of 0.98 percent. In other words, the *compounded annual return* is almost 1 percent lower than the *average annual return* for the higher-risk all stock portfolio. The lower-risk wiser diversification portfolio with the same average return of 7.5 percent has a smaller volatility drag of approximately 0.35 percent. The *compounded annual return* is only

0.35 percent lower than the *average annual return* for the lower-risk wiser diversification portfolio. This is why investors care about compounded annual return.

In the above example, portfolios with the same expected average return have different compounded annual expected returns because of volatility drag. The portfolio with lower expected volatility has a higher expected compounded return at the same level of average return. Your free lunch is being served. It comes with cake (high expected return), and you get to eat it (lower expected risk).

Volatility drag, at its simplest, is the reduction in performance over time caused by higher volatility, and it increases as volatility increases. Two investments with the same average annual return could end up with significantly different ending values after a period of time because of the negative pull of higher volatility. Volatility drag is present in all investments that have any degree of volatility, but the magnitude of the negative effect increases in line with increases in volatility. Take, for example, a portfolio worth $100,000 with a -10 percent return in the first month followed by a 10 percent return in the second month. Simple arithmetic reveals an average return of zero; however, the average compounded return is actually less. At the end of the second month, you wind up with only $99,000, as $1,000 is lost to volatility drag. Because of continual fluctuations and movement in assets, the difference increases between the average rate of return and the rate at which your money compounds, and you wind up losing significant amounts of money to volatility drag.

So, how do you control volatility drag? You can control it and keep it in check by creating a diverse portfolio with lower volatility. As shown in Figures 7.3 and 7.4, the more volatile a portfolio, the more you will lose to volatility drag. This is because the higher the volatility of a portfolio, the more frequent and more sizeable fluctuations will be, resulting in more losses to drag. One of the numerous advantages of wiser diversification is portfolios containing many unique asset classes with low correlations to each other. This diversification results in lower volatility for the overall diversified portfolio, and this keeps compounded returns higher and volatility drag lower, if all else is equal.

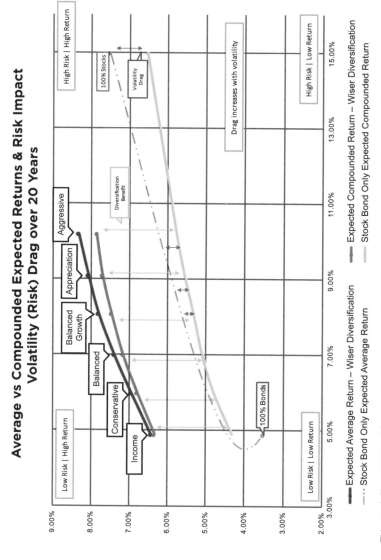

Figure 7.4

OPTIMIZATION VERSUS DIVERSIFICATION
TO REDUCE RISK

Modern Portfolio Theory (MPT) is the center of our firm's portfolio strategy modeling and optimization. Simple diversification reduces risk by mixing assets. Optimization takes into account how assets move together (their correlations) and their respective expected returns. The utilization of low-correlation or uncorrelated asset classes does wonders for risk reduction. MPT is the most widely accepted framework for managing diversified investment portfolios; however, MPT has its limitations around correlations and volatility, because correlations tend to go up as markets go down and volatilities go up.

Optimization is a complex mathematical problem that demands sophisticated computer analytics. I utilize Bloomberg Portfolio Optimizer for this difficult part of building an optimized portfolio. Wiser diversification with low-correlation asset classes tends to improve a portfolio's risk-adjusted expected return profile.

Wiser diversification depends on utilizing asset classes that often have little or no correlation with each other. For example, the reinsurance market, which is mainly dependent on accidents and natural disasters, has minimal correlation with the stock market. So, if there is a downturn in the reinsurance market, your stocks will likely be unaffected, and vice versa. Therefore, if a portfolio is filled with uncorrelated or low-correlation assets such as stocks, bonds, reinsurance, real estate, alternative lending, real assets, and VRP harvesting, the overall risk decreases. That does not mean each asset is low risk; the overall risk of a diversified portfolio of multiple, uncorrelated assets is lower than a 100 percent stock portfolio. Figure 7.4 is an asset class correlation matrix that I use, where pairs of assets' estimated correlation shows how closely together those asset classes move. Zero indicates no correlation (i.e., the assets have no effect on one another), and one indicates is perfect correlation (i.e., the two assets always move together). You can see that, in the real world, there are not many zeros or negatives; hence, real world diversification does not enjoy the hypothetical zero correlation between multiple asset classes.

Correlations are only part of the optimization process, which trades risk and reward. The expected return and the associated risk are important elements as well. Expected return and expected risk are not forecasted returns or risks but are only statistical definitions for modeling purposes. The above is not meant to be a full or complete discussion of all the risks involved in investing, because that is beyond the scope of any one chapter or the book. Many of the risks involved in investing are not specifically named above exist nonetheless. Although the asset class assumptions below are not forecasts, they are helpful in judging the relative attraction of asset classes, especially as they are mixed together into a globally diversified portfolio. To be clear, these assumptions will not be correct and will be off over extended periods of time, and actual results will differ materially and could very well be negative (losses) for any or all of the asset classes. The asset class assumptions on risk and return provide only reasonable guesstimates that allow for portfolio construction to take place with the benefit of a mathematical optimizer. Again, they are not forecasts.

Asset Class Correlation Matrix

	Cash	Bonds	Alternative Lending	US Stocks	US Small Cap Stocks	Developed Intl Stocks	Emerging Markets Stocks	All Asset VRP Harvesting	Alternatives Other	Equity Variance Risk Premium	Reinsurance	Real Estate and Real Assets
Cash	1.00											
Bonds	0.11	1.00										
Alternative Lending	-0.18	0.21	1.00									
US Stocks	-0.16	-0.08	0.60	1.00								
US Small Cap Stocks	-0.15	-0.13	0.50	0.92	1.00							
Developed International Stocks	-0.09	0.04	0.60	0.88	0.78	1.00						
Emerging Markets Stocks	-0.06	0.03	0.50	0.78	0.70	0.85	1.00					
All Asset VRP Harvesting	-0.03	-0.06	0.10	0.12	0.15	0.20	0.25	1.00				
Alternatives Other	-0.12	0.02	0.40	0.71	0.66	0.77	0.77	0.10	1.00			
Equity Variance Risk Premium	-0.12	-0.01	0.55	0.96	0.85	0.97	0.87	0.18	0.78	1.00		
Reinsurance	0.05	0.18	0.20	0.13	0.08	0.15	0.14	0.10	0.24	0.15	1.00	
Real Estate and Real Assets	0.00	0.26	0.30	0.35	0.43	0.40	0.45	0.05	0.20	0.40	0.12	1.00

Figure 7.5

Asset Class Assumptions—October 2018

NOMINAL EXPECTED LONG-TERM AVERAGE RETURNS (OVER 10 TO 20 YEARS)

Asset Class	Long-term Expected Return	Expected Risk
Cash	2.65%	0.1%
Bonds	3.50%	4.9%
Alternative Lending	6.50%	5.0%
US Stocks	7.50%	15.0%
US Small Cap Stocks	8.50%	18.0%
Developed International Stocks	8.25%	17.0%
Emerging Markets Stocks	11.00%	23.0%
All Asset VRP Harvesting	8.50%	10.0%
Alternatives Other	8.25%	11.0%
Equity Variance Risk Premium	8.00%	12.0%
Reinsurance	8.70%	9.0%
Real Estate and Real Assets	8.00%	6.5%

Figure 7.6

Research has consistently found that the best way to maximize expected returns across every level of expected risk is to combine asset classes rather than individual securities, because individual securities of the same asset class are highly correlated. For instance, all stocks generally move in the same direction on a daily, monthly, and yearly basis.

Optimization requires identifying a broad set of diversified asset classes to serve as the building blocks for your portfolio. We analyze potential asset classes' long-term historical behavior across different economic scenarios and provide reasonable go-forward estimates for characteristics of each asset class, such as correlations to other asset classes, expected returns, and expected risks. Estimates are not projections but are merely statistical devices to utilize in the optimization. A positive expected return does not mean the asset will have a positive return, nor is it a forecast of a positive return. See full disclaimer at the beginning of book.

Global Asset Classes
TRILLIONS OF DOLLARS

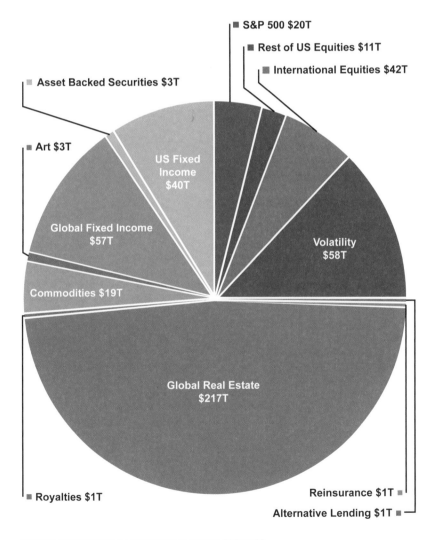

SOURCE: STONE RIDGE, ILLUMINATING THE PATH FORWARD

Global Equities and Fixed Income
TRILLIONS OF DOLLARS

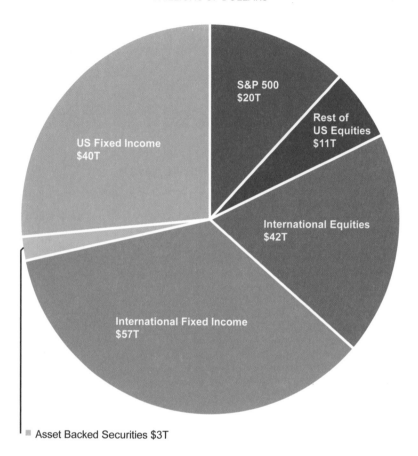

S&P 500
$20T

Rest of
US Equities
$11T

US Fixed Income
$40T

International Equities
$42T

International Fixed Income
$57T

Asset Backed Securities $3T

SOURCE: STONE RIDGE, ILLUMINATING THE PATH FORWARD

US Equities and Fixed Income
TRILLIONS OF DOLLARS

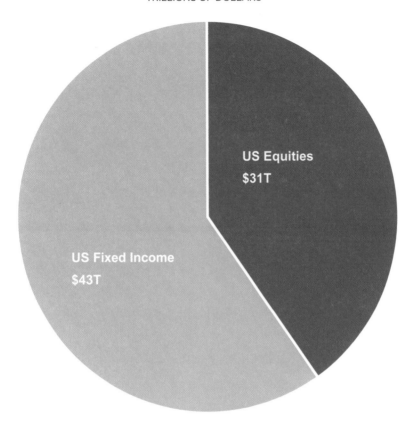

SOURCE: STONE RIDGE, ILLUMINATING THE PATH FORWARD

Figure 7.7

These pie charts from chapter 2 show specific asset classes and depicts how much of the global marketplace they occupy. While many investors and advisers act as if the S&P 500 is the end-all be-all, as you can see here, it is merely a fraction of the global asset classes. Even when you add other US stocks and the US fixed-income market, which contains instruments such as bonds, US asset classes add up to just about $74 trillion, which again is just scraping the surface of the massive global market totaling about $500 trillion. Broadening into international stocks and bonds still misses out on about two-thirds of total global assets. Some of these other asset classes could further diversify and potentially improve a portfolio. A wide range of global asset classes, ranging from reinsurance to real estate to timberland and many more, create a diversified global portfolio. Utilizing more of the opportunities (asset classes) in the global market, rather than just a fraction of them, allows you to build a portfolio with higher expected returns while utilizing diversification and optimization to manage risk. Such portfolios are stronger over the full course of an economic cycle and/or the period including a full bear/bull market cycle.

Asset classes fall under four broad categories: cash, bonds, stocks, and alternatives. Cash is known for safety, but in the current interest rate environment, it does not really provide a significant return; hence, is used only tactically for short periods or for liquidity needs. Bonds and bond-like securities are the most important income-producing asset classes for income-seeking investors. Although bonds have lower return expectations than stocks, they provide a cushion and potential reserve for redeployment to stocks or other investments with higher expected return during periodic financial market sell-offs. Bonds show modest volatility and low correlation with global stock markets. Stocks have higher long-term expected returns but have higher risk and will have periods of significant losses. Stocks, however, do have some long-run inflation protection, because they represent ownership in real businesses that will grow in nominal terms in an inflationary environment. Stocks are tax-advantaged investments, as long-term capital gains and dividends receive preferential tax treatment, and capital gain taxes are deferred until the stock is sold. ETFs and mutual funds enjoy some of this benefit, although individual stocks are more tax advantaged. Alternatives, as we use the term, are assets that have not been typically available to most investors. Alternatives will have at least one, if not all, of the following attributes compared to stocks, bonds, or cash: low correlation, low volatility, or low risk/return profile.

Asset Classes and Their Functions

Asset Class	Benefits
Cash	Safety
Bonds	Yield, diversification, and safety
Alternative Lending	High yield, low interest rate risk
US Stocks	Capital growth, long-run inflation protection, tax efficiency
US Small Cap Stocks	Capital growth, long-run inflation protection, tax efficiency
Developed International Stocks	Capital growth, long-run inflation protection, tax efficiency
Emerging Markets Stocks	Capital growth, long-run inflation protection
All Asset VRP Harvesting	Diversification and high expected return
Alternatives Other	Diversification and modest expected return
Equity Variance Risk Premium	High expected return with lower than stock market volatility
Reinsurance	Diversification, high expected yield, low interest rate risk
Real Estate and Real Assets	Income, diversification, inflation protection

Figure 7.8

A brief summary of asset classes and their descriptions follows:

Cash—Cash and equivalents are investment securities that are short-term, have high credit quality, and are highly liquid. These securities have a low-risk, low-return profile. Cash equivalents include US government Treasury bills, bank CDs, bankers' acceptances, corporate commercial paper, and other money market instruments.

Bonds—Bonds are debts issued by governments or corporations to fund various spending programs or business activities. They can vary in credit quality from very highly rated, investment-grade government or corporate bonds, which offer lower yields in exchange for greater safety, down to very poorly rated speculative ("junk") bonds, which provide much higher yields but with a much higher risk of default. United States government bonds currently offer yields that are at or near historical lows and may produce returns that barely keep up with inflation (or even fall behind and fail to produce positive real returns).

Alternative lending—Alternative lending is a relatively new asset class available for investment and is made up of loans made to consumers or businesses by investors, outside of a traditional bank loan. They are sometimes referred to as peer-to-peer (P2P) lending. Alternative lending currently offers yields that are attractive relative to corporate or government bonds while also providing lower interest rate risk due to shorter maturities. It does have credit risk, as some borrowers will default.

US stocks—Domestic (US) stocks represent ownership in US-based corporations. We expect US stocks (as businesses) to grow with the economy while being affected by investor sentiment, liquidity, and valuation.

US small-cap stocks—These are ownership shares of US-based corporations with smaller market capitalizations. The definition of a small market cap can vary but is generally defined as between $200 million and $2 billion. Small-cap stocks traditionally exhibit greater volatility than large-cap stocks.

International stocks, developed countries—International stocks from developed countries refer to equity shares of corporations based in foreign (relative to the US) but developed nations. The list of "developed" nations can vary but generally includes much of Europe, as well as Japan,

Canada, and Australia. Developed nations' stocks are generally assumed to have somewhat higher levels of risk than US stocks.

International stocks, emerging countries—International stocks from emerging countries are equity shares of corporations based in foreign (relative to the US) nations that are on their way to reaching developed status. They are often referred to as *developing countries* or *emerging markets*. The list of "emerging" nations can vary but generally includes China, much of Southeast Asia, South America, Russia, India, parts of Africa, other parts of Asia, the Middle East, and Eastern Europe. Emerging markets' stocks are generally assumed to have higher levels of risk than US or developed international stocks.

All Asset VRP—This refers to the "variance risk premium" that can be harvested across a wide variety of asset classes. VRP is a phenomenon seen in options markets where the implied volatility is greater than the realized volatility, on average and over time. This means that the writers or sellers of options ("insurance" against unwanted moves in the price of an asset), on average and over time, realize a positive return because buyers of options are willing to pay a premium for that protection. By systematically writing puts and calls (options that protect against drops or gains in an asset price) across a great variety of assets classes, one can expect to generate a positive return over time that has a very low to zero correlation to the equity or bond markets.

Alternatives—Alternatives are a broad category used to describe investments that do not fall into the three traditional asset types (stocks, bonds, and cash). Alternative investments can include the following: hedge funds, managed futures, real estate, commodities, currencies, long/short funds, and other complex strategies. Alternatives have traditionally been held by institutional investors and high-net-worth individuals, but new products and vehicles are beginning to allow more investors to participate in this space.

Equity VRP—Equity VRP is a subset of VRP discussed above; but is focused on only VRPs harvested from the equities markets. In this asset class, we also include strategies that both have an equity VRP component and participate in equity market returns. These assets participate in the returns of the stock market. A covered call strategy, where call options are sold on stock portfolio positions, is the most common example of a strategy that would fit in this asset class.

Reinsurance—Reinsurance, broadly, is the practice of insurers transferring portions of risk from their portfolios of policies to other parties via some form of agreement to reduce their risk exposure from an insurance claim. As an asset class, *reinsurance* refers to investors providing capital to insurers through investments with reinsurers and other vehicles, including catastrophe (CAT) bonds, in exchange for a return or share in the premiums generated. The insurance is tied to a variety of possible events, such as hurricanes, earthquakes, aviation or maritime disasters, losses related to crops or livestock, flooding, and so on. By their nature, natural disasters are uncorrelated with movements in investment markets—a crash in the stock markets cannot cause an earthquake, and an earthquake would generally not cause the stock market to crash. Furthermore, these natural disasters are internally uncorrelated—an airplane crashing will not cause an earthquake or vice versa. This lack of correlation with other investments allows reinsurance to act as a diversifier in a portfolio, meaning that when the stock market is down, these investments move independently and may be up, the same, or even down as well—but are not based on moves in the stock market. This diversification effect lowers the overall risk of a portfolio.

Real estate and real assets—Real estate and real assets refer, in this case, to investments in physical or tangible assets such as property, buildings, equipment, pipelines, timberland, infrastructure, precious metals, commodities, agricultural real estate, and oil and gas properties. These investments typically exhibit a lower correlation with stocks and bonds and are generally well-suited for inflationary times, because they have a tendency to outperform financial assets during such periods.

Expected Benefits of Wiser Diversification

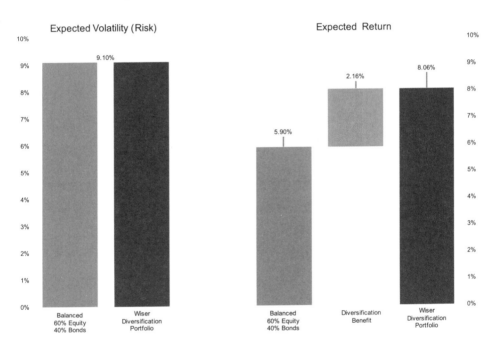

Investing in stocks, bonds, and other assets which present various forms of risk to investors could result in losses and positive returns are not guaranteed. Diversification only reduces risk of capital loss but does not eliminate this risk. Measures of expected return and/or expected risk are not forecasts of returns or risks but are only statistical definitions for modeling purposes based upon financial and statistical analyses. Past performance is no indication of future results, and all investments or assets could lose value in the future due to a variety of financial factors. Due to volatility exhibited in various markets, including but not limited to stocks, bonds and other forms of investable assets these markets may not perform in a similar manner in the future. Among risks which can affect value, financial assets are also exposed to potential inflation and liquidity risks. Investors may experience different results in any chosen investment strategy or portfolio depending on the time and placement of capital into any assets associated thereto. The performance of a specific individual client account may vary substantially from the performance results reflected above. Diverified strategyies are constructed to diversify from an all-bond portfolio, directed toward investment among assets that may largely, though not necessarily completely, be non-bond alternatives. Investors are cautioned that they should carefully consider fully diversifying their total personal investment allocations to incorporate a variety of investment assets which also may include stocks, stock mutual funds and ETFs, international assets, bonds and fixed income instruments (where appropriate), and other non-stock/bond investments (e.g., without limitation, Real Estate and other assets).

Figure 7.9

Figure 7.9 shows how all this potentially works in when we build a hypothetical portfolio utilizing diversifying assets and wiser optimization. As opposed to using bonds to lower risk (and dramatically lower expected return), diversifying assets accomplish similar risk reduction but do not have the painful problem of much lower returns.

──────────── **Your Takeaway** ────────────

Wiser diversification is a combination of several opportunities:

- More diversifying asset classes

- Optimization versus stock/bond-only diversification

- Asset classes with low or modest correlations

- Minimizing volatility drag to improve compounded annual return

Please see risk disclosure and details at the beginning of the book.

CHAPTER 8

The Rise of the Independent RIA

*"Having lived long, I have experienced many instances of
being obliged by better information or fuller consideration
to change opinions, even on important subjects, which
I once thought right, but found to be otherwise."*

—BENJAMIN FRANKLIN

ACCORDING TO KAREN BARR, President and CEO of the Investment Adviser Association, "The growth of the federally registered investment adviser (RIA) industry has been remarkably robust since 2001, with record high numbers of advisers virtually every year. Total industry regulatory assets under management (RAUM), as well as numbers of clients served, have also grown substantially. This demonstrates that the industry is flexible and resilient, with the ability to adapt and evolve to meet the demands of changing client demographics and market trends. And investment advisers remain a powerful provider of high-quality jobs to the economy, especially in small businesses."

Accessing diversifying assets is most easily accomplished through an RIA or a broker that utilizes an RIA to get access to these strategies. Some individual investors are not aware of the RIA industry so this chapter is for them.

Following the financial crisis of 2008, the popularity of non-wirehouse brokerage firms and independent RIAs has continued to grow each year in terms of total client assets. Now, after several years of slower growth, client assets have returned to a more normalized 9 percent compound annual growth rate from year-end 2008 to year-end 2017. As a result, overall growth of client assets reached 19 percent, buoyed by a 22 percent total return in the S&P 500. Many investors now work with an RIA, either directly or through a financial adviser. However, a lot of clients do not work with an RIA, do not know they exist, and/or do not understand the difference between an RIA and a wirehouse broker working for one of the heavily advertised wealth management firms.

Year	2012	2013	2014	2015	2016	2017	2018
No. of Advisers	10,511	10,533	10,895	11,473	11,847	12,172	12,578

SOURCE: INVESTMENT ADVISOR ASSOCIATION, 2018 EVOLUTION/REVOLUTION

Figure 8.1

This chart shows the increasing numbers of RIAs since 2012.

According to the Investment Adviser Act of 1940, an RIA is a "person or firm that, for compensation, is engaged in the act of providing advice, making recommendations, issuing reports or furnishing analyses on securities, either directly or through publications."

An RIA is registered either with the SEC or, for smaller firms, with state securities authorities. Because they have a fiduciary responsibility to their clients, RIAs must, above all else, act in those clients' best interests. Many people believed, especially in the past, that acting in a client's best interest was a given when working in the financial services industry. That is not the case. Only RIAs have a legal fiduciary responsibility. Others answer to what is known as the *suitability standard.*

The suitability standard details only that the broker-dealer has to reasonably believe that any recommendations made are suitable for clients in terms of an individual client's financial needs, objectives, and circumstances. Furthermore, a broker's primary duty and loyalty belong to that broker's employer and not necessarily to the client. This is not to say that every broker ignores fiduciary responsibility, only that the suitability standard is not as stringent as the fiduciary standard regarding what a financial professional must reveal and whom that person must serve.

Four kinds of RIA firms exist in the investment market. The most common are RIAs who take care of individual investors and outsources investment management to ETFs, mutual funds, and asset-management-oriented RIAs. The second are asset management RIAs, who provide investment services to other RIAs, independent broker-dealers, and the wirehouses. The third are money-manager-only RIAs, who pick individual stocks and bonds for their clients but do not use third-party asset managers and do not sell their services to other financial advisers. Last are combination firms, which provide at least two (and sometimes all three) of the capabilities described above.

Investors or clients are often confused when trying to distinguish who does what. Not only are there fiduciary RIAs and suitability brokers; there are also multiple flavors of each. It is no wonder that the investing public often does not know the type of financial advisers they have or are considering hiring. The breadth of capabilities is almost as large as in the food business. The corner deli and the corn farmer are both in the food business but have very different functions. The investment business is similar, but clients are less readily able to distinguish the nuances of its many varieties.

FIDUCIARY RESPONSIBILITY

Because of their commitment to fiduciary responsibility, RIAs are required to disclose all material risks associated with analysis methods used to determine suitability, as well as any unusual risk that may be involved in a specific investment security or strategy. RIAs must also disclose—in clear language, in a client brochure—whether they have a relationship or arrangement, including participation or an interest in any client transaction, that could present a conflict of interest. From the beginning of the working relationship, a potential client is aware of all circumstances that could influence a transaction, even if those circumstances are not actually influencing the RIA. The proverbial cards are on the table, and the transparency creates an environment of trust in which the client and the RIA will conduct business. This is the environment many investors prefer today.

One 2018 survey found that 78 percent of participating RIA firms expected their assets under management to rise in 2018. Nearly half expected their assets to grow faster than in 2017.[15] Sixty-five

---

[15] "RIAs expect faster asset growth in 2018," *InvestmentNews*, January 9, 2018, http://www.investmentnews.com/article/20180109/FREE/180109940/rias-expect-faster-asset-growth-in-2018.

percent of those interviewed gained new clients the previous year. Revenues of those interviewed grew, on average, by 15 percent during the second half of 2017, and assets under management grew by 16 percent.

PUBLIC TRUST

The rise of independent RIAs has been supported by "the Big 3": TD Ameritrade, Charles Schwab, and Fidelity Investments. These firms provide safekeeping, custody, and trading capabilities to clients of independent RIAs. They also provide leading-edge technology that allows RIAs to interface with these custodians for reporting and trading. Moreover, "the Big 3" provide client referrals to the independent RIAs.

In this environment, clients who need help with investing or planning are referred to an independent RIA who will take care of the client. The assets stay with the referring custodian, and the RIA generally pays a fee to the referring custodian. "The Big 3" are growing faster than the wirehouses, and oftentimes, the investing public trusts "the Big 3" firms more than the big wirehouses.[16] By using "Big 3" branded custodians, the RIA industry gets real trading and custodian benefits, along with additional reassurance for clients that their assets are in custody at a big brand name. The combination of brand, service, lower sales pressure,

> The combination of brand, service, lower sales pressure, and the utilization of independent RIAs who provide true fiduciary services has separated "the Big 3" from their wirehouse competition.

---

16   Cyril Tuohy, "Wirehouse Assets Sliding to Burgeoning RIAs," Insurance-NewsNet.com, June 25, 2018, https://insurancenewsnet.com/innarticle/wirehouse-assets-sliding-to-burgeoning-rias#.W_MIknpKiis.

and the utilization of independent RIAs who provide true fiduciary services has separated "the Big 3" from their wirehouse competition.

Investors perceive RIAs and independent broker-dealers to be superior, and many wirehouse advisers also recognize this trend in perception. In 2016, according to *InvestmentNews* data, the four wirehouses saw $70 billion in assets controlled by advisers move to other firms, though close to $30 billion of that amount, or 43 percent, moved from one wirehouse to another. Still, a net of $40 billion left for other channels, including RIAs. Why did those funds and those people leave?

According to a 2017 survey by Cerulli Associates, 69 percent of breakaway advisers—those moving from a wirehouse or regional firm to a pure or hybrid RIA or independent broker-dealer—said that a "desire for greater independence" was a "major factor" in their decision. At the same time, 56 percent said "concerns about quality of broker-dealer's culture" was a "major factor" in deciding to move.[17]

The advantages of moving from a wirehouse often outweigh the advantages of staying. No longer can the legacy software of the past compete with innovative and rapidly changing software available to independents, who can update and change at will. But the reasons for the rise of the RIA go far beyond technology. Indeed, they go to heart of the public's perception—and expectations—of those in the financial services industry. Public trust and lack of it are major components in the movement away from the wirehouses.

In writing this book, I interviewed author of *The New Profession*, Bob Veres, of Inside Information. When I asked him why RIAs were growing faster than wirehouses, he said this:

---

17   Bruce Kelly, "Independent broker-dealers are stepping up their game on recruiting from the wirehouses," *InvestmentNews*, January 27, 2018, http://www.investmentnews.com/article/20180127/FREE/180129946/ independent-broker-dealers-are-stepping-up-their-game-on-recruiting.

"The first and most important reason is that consumers overwhelmingly prefer a consultant to a salesperson when they are selecting...*anything*. And increasingly, they realize that the brokerage firms are in the sales business, no matter what misleading label is placed on their business cards. The decades-long rising awareness of conflicts, sales quotas, and hidden fees has caused constant, incremental shifts in consumer loyalty from brokers to advisors."

RIA AND INDEPENDENT PREFERENCE

More and more people in the financial services profession are moving from the pressures of quotas to the independent RIA community. Pressure combined with public disrespect and distrust can taint the promise of any success, however grand, in these heavily bottom-line-driven environments.

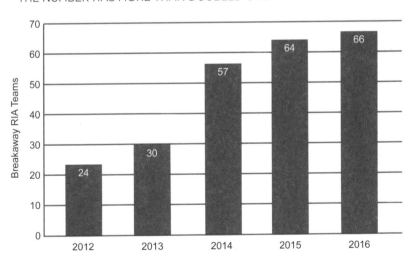

Breakaway Teams Joining RIAs at Record Highs
THE NUMBER HAS MORE THAN DOUBLED OVER THE PAST FIVE YEARS

SOURCE: SEC DATABASE, COMPANY REPORTS, MEDIA REPORTS, ECHELON ANALYSIS

Figure 8.2

Veres tells audiences attending his presentations that many brokers leave the wirehouses to work with independent broker-dealers; this is still a sales role, but one more independent and governed by their consciences. "If you held a gun to their heads and ordered them to go back to the brokerage world, they would say, 'Pull the trigger.' Similarly, there is a constant inflow from independent broker-dealers to fee-only planning firms (either an established firm or starting their own). If you held a gun to the new fee-only planner and said, 'Go back and get your sales licenses and start earning commissions,' they have the same response, 'Pull the trigger.'"

IMPACT OF THE FIDUCIARY RULE: POSITIVE OR NEGATIVE?

Many in the financial services industry have been concerned about the effects of the Department of Labor (DOL) fiduciary rule (officially "Definition of the Term 'Fiduciary'; Conflict of Interest Rule—Retirement Investment Advice"). The rule was designed to make *all* financial professionals who provided retirement planning advice or who worked with retirement plans accountable to the fiduciary standard—as opposed to the suitability standard, which offers far more latitude.

Shortly after taking office in 2017, President Donald Trump asked for a review of the fiduciary rule. Originally scheduled to be phased in from April 10, 2017 to January 1, 2018, the rule was instead invalidated by the 5th Circuit Court of Appeals, citing "unreasonableness" and saying that the DOL's implementation of the rule constitutes "an arbitrary and capricious exercise of administrative power." The newly installed DOL leaders have declined to appeal the consumer protections created by the last DOL. "Pending further review," the DOL would not be enforcing the 2016 fiduciary rule as of March 2018, and the 5th Circuit Court of Appeals confirmed its decision to vacate the rule on June 21, 2018.

Those arguing in favor of the rule pointed out how much money investors paid to commission-earning brokers. For instance, a 2015 report from the White House Council of Economic Advisers estimates that conflicts of interests by brokers annually cost retirement investors up to $17 billion.[18]

Those against the rule pointed out the 22.5 percent drop in financial advisers in the UK after the 2011 passing a similar rule. They argued that the rule could unfairly affect smaller and independent retirement advisers, who might not be able to afford complying with the new regulations. Many preferred the status quo of the suitability standard, arguing that conforming to the fiduciary standard would cost too much. In fairness to those arguing that commissions should be allowed, some clients—generally those in the accumulation phase—do have circumstances where they benefit from the advice of a salesperson who receives a commission. The issue is not as binary as some portray, but lack of a fiduciary rule makes opportunities for unscrupulous sales practices more common. Most financial advisers, even when not officially governed by the fiduciary rule, put their clients' interests first, and it is unfortunate that the industry is tarred by a minority of bad actors.

> Those arguing in favor of the rule pointed out how much money investors paid to commission-earning brokers.

---

18 Matthew Frankel, "The Fiduciary Rule: Pros and Cons," The Motley Fool, February 3, 2017, https://www.fool.com/retirement/2017/02/03/the-fiduciary-rule-pros-and-cons.aspx.

What those arguments did was shine a very bright light on how those in the investment business earned their fees. Writing for *Forbes*, David Trainer points out that after the original proposal, "some of the largest advisor groups in the world have made changes to better serve clients. A large wirehouse moved clients from commission-based accounts to fee-based ones.[19]

"Even if it is never fully enacted, the DOL rule has done incalculable harm to the brokerage community," says Bob Veres. "The wirehouse trade organization, Securities Industry and Financial Markets Association (SIFMA), was forced to argue, right there on paper, that its brokers and representatives were merely in a sales role whenever they interacted with consumers, and therefore the rule should not apply to them. The hullabaloo over whether the rule should be enacted made consumers much more aware of the fiduciary standard, and in general what advisors were sitting on the same side of the table as they were when they sought advice."

THE FUTURE STANDARD: FIDUCIARY

Knowledge of the fiduciary standard has indeed increased public awareness of how people in the financial services community are compensated. Regardless of the status of the DOL rule, trust has become an even greater issue in investment than it was previously. Ultimately, as always, the public will decide, and the industry will follow. That is what has been happening, and for the reasons presented here, the rise of the independent RIA will continue. Investors have changed. The investing client wants more transparency, and they want to pay for

---

19   Mary Hayes Weier, "8 Takeaways from the Wall Street Journal CFO Network Annual Meeting," *Forbes*, June 20, 2018, https://www.forbes.com/sites/workday/2018/06/20/8-takeaways-from-the-wall-street-journal-cfo-network-annual-meeting/#3f4b6f8e3765.

sound advice, not for a salesperson's shrewdness and finesse. When what the public wants and what an advisor wants align, the transition to RIAs will only continue to increase. Some sales-oriented organizations are opting to utilize asset management RIAs for the delivery of some or all of their investment services. This model makes a lot of sense, as the sales organization is set to provide client service to thousands or millions of clients, while the asset management RIA can bring objective and sophisticated investment solutions to the client on a fee-only basis.

——————— Your Takeaway ———————

- An RIA is registered either with the SEC or, for smaller firms, with state securities authorities.

- Fiduciary responsibility means that, from the beginning of the working relationship, an RIA's potential client is aware of all circumstances that could influence a transaction.

- The suitability standard details only that the broker-dealer has to reasonably believe that any recommendations made are suitable for the client.

- "The Big 3" have supported the rise of independent RIAs.

- More investors have realized that brokerage firms are in the sales business.

- Emphasis on quotas and sales pressure has influenced many brokers to move to the independent RIA community.

- The DOL fiduciary rule, which was designed to make all financial professionals accountable to the fiduciary standard, was vacated on June 21, 2018.

- Nevertheless, the DOL rule has increased consumers' awareness of the fiduciary standard and about the compensation structure of financial professionals.

CHAPTER 9

Surviving the Next Big Bear

"If passion drives, let reason hold the reins."

—BENJAMIN FRANKLIN

"THE TERM 'BEAR MARKET' is the opposite of a 'bull market,' or a market in which prices for securities are rising or will expect to rise. It is named for the way in which a bear attacks its prey — swiping its paws downward. This is why markets with falling stock prices are called bear markets. Just like the bear market, the bull market is named after the way in which the bull attacks by thrusting its horns up into the air. While there is no agreed upon definition of what makes a bear market, it's generally accepted that a bear market is characterized by a drop of 20 percent or more over a two-month period" from the most recent highs.[20] Bear markets generally move faster on the downside than bull markets on the upside and usually last around a year or two. Bull markets have much longer durations. Bear markets are shorter, sharper, and more violent.

Low employment, low disposable income, and a drop in business profits can signal a slowing economy. Other signs include changes in the tax rate and loss of investor confidence. The different phases of the transition to a bear market include the following:

1. High prices and positive investor sentiment generally mark the top of a bull market.

2. The market starts to roll over as some investors sell and take profits.

3. As prices start to decline, investors wonder if it just a correction or the start of something worse. Only after stock prices fall sharply is it clear a bear market has started.

4. The start of bear markets generally lead recessions and corporate profits declines by six to eighteen months. Some investors begin to panic. Trading volume tends to increase.

5. After the high-volume panic, stock prices start to stabilize or drop more slowly. Low prices begin to attract value investors. Stabilization attracts more buyers, and the market eventually bottoms.

The time to prepare for the next bear market is before it arrives. That would be now. Recent bear markets were caused by a decline in housing prices in 2008, the internet bubble in 2000, the Iraqi invasion of Kuwait in 1990, and rising interest rates and portfolio insurance

---

20 "Bear Market," Investopedia, https://www.investopedia.com/terms/b/bearmarket.asp#ixzz5Or5A0Ng3.

in 1987. Regardless of what leads to the next one, remember this rule of stock investing: there will be another bear market, and most investors will not see it coming.

PROTECT YOUR CAPITAL

At the time of this writing, the vast majority of investors have only stocks and bonds, because until recently, the items discussed in this book were not readily available in sizes and minimums that would allow most people to utilize them.

In the methodology we have discussed throughout this book, you reduce your bond exposure, reduce your stock exposure, and mix in several other uncorrelated or low-correlation assets. That is at the heart of this strategy, and it lowers your year-to-year risk considerably, because you are not concentrated in any one asset class. That said, in a booming stock market year, diversified portfolios will most definitely lag behind an all-stock portfolio. Although diversifying strategies will have some bonds, both the bond and the equity portions would be lower than a typical balanced portfolio of 60 percent stocks and 40 percent bonds. The diversifying assets could replace some exposure to both. How much replacement of each would depend on your risk tolerance, time horizon, and income needs.

> In the methodology we have discussed throughout this book, you reduce your bond exposure, reduce your stock exposure, and mix in several other, uncorrelated or low-correlation assets.

As a result, wiser diversification ends up having lower expected risk, higher expected return, or possibly a little of both in comparison to a stock-and-bond-only balanced portfolio. When the stock market goes down, some of the diversifying, uncorrelated assets might go up, or might not go down nearly as much as stocks. Their returns are uncorrelated with the stock market, meaning that they are not connected to the market. That's the good news. The returns of uncorrelated assets are generally independent.

What does that mean to you? For starters, you are protecting your capital. Diversification is going to help you withstand a bear market without having to move too much money into low-yielding bonds and giving up a lot of expected return. As we discussed earlier, if you reduce the size of your losses or expected risk, your expected compound return should improve.

SLEEP BETTER AT NIGHT

No one wants to be owned by their investments, and wondering whether yours are going to deprive you of your capital and your plans for a comfortable retirement can keep you awake many nights. Even when the market is heading down, you should be able to sleep through it, knowing that part of your money is not exposed to stocks, as opposed to having 100 percent of your money in stocks.

Protect capital. Compound faster. Sleep better. If you've made it through the book this far, you understand that bonds are, at best, a low expected return with significant interest rate risk or, at worst, broken compared to where they were thirty years ago. Times change, and today, there are wiser ways for you to invest, because interval funds give you potential exposure to asset classes that previously required a big minimum investment.

NOT READILY AVAILABLE—UNTIL NOW

You also know that a bond substitute or reduction segment has the potential to improve your income stream compared to a traditional bond portfolio while providing some protection in a down market. This segment involves the utilization of truly low or uncorrelated assets—reinsurance, private real estate, alternative lending, timberland, infrastructure, and VRP harvesting strategies—to increase yield, increase diversification, and reduce risk.

Many have been skeptical of this diversification, but that is because they haven't heard about it, and they haven't had it available. I understand that. Someone tells you that you can pick up two extra percentage points of expected return at every level of expected risk, and you should be skeptical. You would be correct in thinking markets aren't supposed to be like that. So, how can it be?

As we've discussed in depth, these asset classes were not readily available until recently in interval funds, and because they are stuck in interval funds, some people just don't want to deal with the additional hassle of illiquidity. You have not heard about wiser diversification for two reasons: only recent broader availability, and the perceived negative of interval funds with limited, not daily, liquidity. Endowment funds, family offices, and wealthy individuals have been utilizing these asset classes for years, because they had enough money to meet the usual $10 million minimum per asset class.

Because bond yields are producing low income in the current environment, and because they have exposure to interest rate risk that could result in losses as rates go higher, we have been working to build a suitable partial substitute for bonds in the form of a truly diversified portfolio that can produce a reasonable expected return. Realizing that the vast majority of Americans don't have access to these diversifying asset classes, we set out to find asset managers who could deliver them at a broader level with lower minimums, so all investors could access them.

With these strategies, we could help all our investors and not just our biggest ones. We could help our clients retire more securely, invest for their kids' college educations, increase portfolio income, and just feel more secure with a portfolio that fluctuates far less than the stock market.

The key to wiser diversification is putting more low-correlation or uncorrelated asset classes into your portfolio to lower your overall portfolio risk. Each asset class may be of high or moderate risk, but wiser diversification means it is unlikely that all of your portfolio assets will have a really big loss at the same time. It's statistically possible, but improbable. I hope I have convinced you that this strategy is not magic and that it is an important consideration for investors today. If I have accomplished these goals, and you want to learn more, you may well be asking, "What's next?"

HOW TO DEPLOY THESE STRATEGIES

At this point, you are probably wondering what your choices are, and that's what I would like to address as I conclude this book. First, this is not a do-it-yourself investment strategy. Indeed, the typical retail investor is not going to get access to most of these strategies. We are working to make these strategies more available to more investors through more financial advisers. This is the main reason for the book. If your current adviser is set up to help you, that is great. If not, contact us, and we will work with your adviser to provide him or her with the capability. Or, if you prefer, we can refer you to a financial adviser who has already added this wiser diversification capability to their skill set.

I wrote this book because I wanted to help investors like you learn more about these little-understood choices and how they can benefit you in today's market and beyond. I wrote it because I believe that diversification—if not the only free lunch—can certainly nourish your portfolio. Most of all, I wrote it because, after all these years, I am passionate about what I do and about helping others prepare for a secure, rewarding future. I sincerely hope that I have been able to provide you with answers or at least stirred your curiosity enough to investigate how wiser diversification can help you.

MY PERSONAL STORY

Now that you've come to know me through this book, I'd like to share some personal information about where I came from and how I found and became passionate about the field of investing.

While growing up in Chattanooga, Tennessee, I attended the McCallie School, played football and baseball, and graduated as co-salutatorian. Obsessed with football, I played into my senior year, fighting a bad back. A season-ending left-knee injury in practice truncated my football-playing days just before my senior season started. This was, strangely, a blessing in disguise, because it prevented additional wear and tear on my body and freed up time for me to focus more on academics. This extra time allowed me to climb up the class rankings and pass several classmates who were, quite frankly, brilliant. In 1981, the McCallie School was still posting all grades and rankings on a board for everyone to see. I was fortunate enough to have the extra time to work on improving my grades and pass some remarkable individuals in the process.

My family was involved in the manufacturing and distribution of office equipment. This was truly a family business that included my mom, my dad, and me. As early as age ten, I would go with my father to trade shows and hang out with him, learning about the wider world of business. I would also help him do some odd-hour installations of said equipment, so I had a lot of business exposure at a young age. For most of my childhood and into my early adult life, I just sort of assumed that I would go into the family business. But like all small businesses, there were good years and some that were not so good. That became particularly acute during the early 1980s recession, when the business ran into significant problems.

I was attending Vanderbilt University at the time, and I took a year off to work in the family business. I had enough background to run the factory, so my father could go out in the field and produce more sales revenue. Fortunately, that strategy worked in the short-term, the business had a recovery, and I was able to go back to school and finish. I was fortunate to have enough advanced placement credits from my high school years to catch up and graduate with my class, even though I missed a full academic year. In 1985, I graduated from Vanderbilt with a bachelor's of science in mathematics and psychology and earned the designation *magna cum laude*.

But that time away from academia taught me more than I could have learned sitting in a lecture hall. It was immersion in the real world, and what I discovered opened my eyes. The first lesson was that hard work in and of itself does not always pay off. My parents worked hard for years, but because of circumstances that were out of their control, the business eventually failed.

Why did it fail? For starters, the office equipment business was very capital intensive, didn't generate a lot of free cash, was easily commoditized, and was hard to differentiate. Worse, increased foreign competition from China and other countries continued nibbling away at the domestic market during the 1980s, reaching 25 percent by 1990, according to a study by Smith and West. That was pretty much the death knell for a large chunk of US furniture manufacturing, and today, the business is more than 50 percent foreign-based. That experience also taught me about the ebbs and flows of business. In truth, even in the best of times, there wasn't a lot of money to be had in the furniture business. We had a few years where we did well, and then it went away for good.

While still working in the family business in 1985, I was only scraping by and knew the time had come for me to investigate other industries. I concluded that three fields seemed especially lucrative: investment, real estate, and insurance. I wrote a summary of the pros and cons of each and submitted it to my dad for discussion—my first real research analyst project. We concluded that, with my math aptitude, investing would be a good career, and off I went.

While at Vanderbilt, I met my wife Anne, and we married as soon as she graduated in 1986. We lived in Atlanta, Durham, New York City, and then, in 1991, Chatham, New Jersey. Our daughter, Cary, was born that same year, and our boys, Gray and Drew, were born in 1994 and 1997 respectively. The 1990s were fantastic. I had a wonderful wife and three great kids, the Atlanta Braves were winning, and yes, there was the big bull market.

Over the years, I had the pleasure of coaching all my kids in various sports but especially baseball. I currently play golf when my back permits, and I also play a version of basketball where jumping is rare and sometimes imperceptible. It provides me with great exercise and mental release. We all enjoy skiing in the Rockies, and with the benefit of modern medicine and a double knee replacement, I can still participate. We still live in Chatham and love the Norman Rockwell feel of the town.

RESOURCES

General knowledge about diversification and using additional asset classes has become ingrained in the investment business. Here are some of the leading original papers that provided thought leadership on these issues:

Bernstein, W.J. *The Intelligent Asset Allocator: How to Build Your Portfolio to Maximize Returns and Minimize Risk.* McGraw-Hill Education, 2000.

Black, F. and R. Litterman. "Global Portfolio Optimization." *Financial Analysts Journal* 48, no. 5 (1992) https://doi.org/10.2469/faj.v48.n5.28.

Brinson, G. P., L. R. Hood, and G. L. Beebower. "Determinants of Portfolio Performance." *Financial Analyst Journal* 51, no. 1 (1986) https://doi.org/10.2469/faj.v51.n1.1869.

Brinson, G. P., B. D. Singer, and G. L. Beebower. "Determinants of Portfolio Performance II: An Update." *Financial Analyst Journal* 47, no. 3 (1991) https://doi.org/10.2469/faj.v47.n3.40.

Fernandez, P., J. P. Carelli, and A. Ortiz. "The Market Portfolio is not efficient: Evidences, consequences and easy to avoid errors." (2016) http://dx.doi.org/10.2139/ssrn.2741083.

Ibbotson, R.G., and P. D. Kaplan. "Does Asset Allocation Policy Explain 40, 90, or 100 Percent of Performance?" *Financial Analyst Journal* 56 (January 2001) https://doi.org/10.2469/faj.v56.n1.2327.

Mandelbrot, B. B., and R. L. Hudson. *The (mis)behavior of markets: A fractal view of risk, ruin, and reward.* London: Profile, 2008.

Markowitz, H. "Portfolio Selection." *Journal of Finances* 7, no. 1 (March 1952): 77–91. https://www.jstor.org/stable/2975974.

Sharpe, W. "Capital Asset Prices: A Theory of Market Equilibrium Under Conditions of Risks." *Journal of Finance* 19, no. 3 (September 1964): 425–442. https://doi.org/10.2307/2977928.

Swensen, D. *Pioneering Portfolio Management: An Unconventional Approach to Institutional Investment.* New York: Free Press, 2000.

Swensen, D. *Unconventional Success: A Fundamental Approach to Personal Investment.* New York: Free Press, 2005.

Stevens, R., Zwick, J., and Cohen, R. Illuminating the Path Forward: Breaking Free from the 60 / 40 Portfolio (2017).